Miracles for Marlee

By

Shannon G. Turner

ISBN: 1-4033-6630-6 (e-book)
ISBN: 1-4033-6631-4 (Paperback)

This book is printed on acid free paper.

1stBooks – rev. 11/06/02

Special Thanks

Special thanks to Scott Page for the beautiful work he did with my photos and cover; to Katie Phillips for editing and helping me believe I can accomplish anything; to Dale Thomson for editing, financial support, and encouraging me to publish this book; to Lenise Wallace for editing and many years of friendship; to my dear friends Chris Bowers, Elaine Osborne, and Debbie Hanson for their years of unconditional love and support; to Kim Fetrow for editing and being such a great neighbor; to Elis Goodey for accompanying me on our amazing trip to China; to Leigh Anne Baseflug and all the staff at Great Wall China Adoption for their first-rate service and professionalism; to all our generous friends and family who helped us bring our little girl home; and especially to Tim, Eric and Marlee for making my life so complete.

INTRODUCTION

I have come to learn that things are done according to God's timing, not our own. They are also done in a way the Lord has planned, not necessarily the way we wish them to happen. The secret is to live each day with faith and prayer, along with a healthy dose of patience and endurance. In the end, a beautiful painting will be unveiled, a life painting containing breathtaking landscapes and vivid colors beyond our imagination.

My name is Shannon Turner. This is the account of our family's journey to adopt our daughter, Marlee. It began in the spring of the year 2000. My husband, Tim, and I were looking forward to celebrating our upcoming 14th wedding anniversary. We lived in Richland, Washington, and both worked in nearby cities. I had been an evidence technician at a local police department for six years and Tim was nearing the end of his 13th year as an English teacher at Kiona-Benton High School in Benton City. Our son, Eric, was nine years old at the time. He reminded us constantly that he was an only child and that he was none too happy about the situation.

For years I felt there was a little girl that was meant to be in our family. One day when Eric was very young, we were driving home from an outing when he said to me from his car seat in the back, "Mom, I hear her!" He took me by surprise because there was no one else in the car. Being only three, though, I thought maybe he had an imaginary friend.

"Hear who, Honey?" I asked.

Eric replied emphatically, "I hear my sister. She's talking to me."

"What did she say?" I curiously asked him.

"She says she's up in heaven and wants to come live with us very soon," he replied.

His sweet sincerity and inspiration, adding to my own yearning and emptiness, made the tears flow freely down my cheeks.

For years, Eric continually prayed that his little sister would come soon. But as time went on, waiting, hoping and praying, I began to think that both Eric's prayers and mine were in vain. It broke my heart to see his disappointment that we could not give him his little sister.

Month after month, my own disappointment grew into a dangerous bitterness. I became angry toward other women for the mere fact that they could have children and I couldn't. I hated every pregnant woman I saw. I even resented my friends who were pregnant. It grew into somewhat of an anti-social anger that consumed me. I continually asked, "Why me? Why can women who don't even want children get pregnant? Why does the Lord give babies to mothers who neglect and abuse them? If they can have a baby, then why won't He give one to me?"

I wondered if perhaps I was being punished for something I had done and wondered why my Heavenly Father was making me go through this. I began to doubt the inspiration I had received through the years that we were meant to have another child. I doubted my personal faith, my own strength, and even the knowledge that my Heavenly Father loved me. My heart became hardened and selfish and I withdrew into my own self-centered pity party.

In 1996, after almost two years of trying to become pregnant using charts, ovulation test kits, thermometers, and all the romantic accessories of trying to have a baby, I finally went to my doctor for direction. He discovered my progesterone level was too low and therefore I was not ovulating well enough to become pregnant. He prescribed a fertility drug to aid in my ovulation.

For eight months I took the fertility pills as prescribed. They made me ultra-emotional, irritable, and just plain hard to be around. I didn't even like being around myself. Even my best friends would cautiously comment that they noticed a difference when I was on them. Each month I convinced myself that I was pregnant; each month I was disappointed when I wasn't. After eight months of an emotional roller coaster and no baby in sight, the doctor took me off the medication.

In the spring of 1997, after experiencing various symptoms for several months, I visited my doctor to tell him my concerns about the pain I was having. He diagnosed my symptoms as a condition called endometriosis, which, he explained, was most likely the reason I had not been able to become pregnant. Fortunately, it could be remedied by surgery. I was comforted by the fact that surgery would fix the problem and then we could get on with our goal of having another baby.

My doctor performed the surgery in May of 1997. I tolerated the recuperation time knowing it was just a matter of time before I would feel better and could put it all behind me. During my post-operative visit with my doctor, however, he informed me I would have to take medication for six months following the surgery to ensure the endometriosis would not return. He explained that the medication would make it impossible for me to become pregnant while I was taking it.

I was devastated! Another six months seemed like an eternity. I had no choice but to develop the attitude that I couldn't change the situation; therefore, I had to accept it and wait another six months. I started the medication in July and continued on it until the end of the year.

January 1, 1998 came, the day I had been waiting for. I was finally off the medication and could get on with my life and our plan for a baby. But within just three months, the symptoms of endometriosis had returned and were worse than the first time. Shooting and stabbing pain that brought me to my knees, constant pressure, and hemorrhaging were a part of my everyday life.

I returned to my doctor, in pain physically and emotionally. He had no choice but to schedule another surgery, this time in April, eleven months after the previous one.

Second verse, same as the first: surgery, medication for six months, and no baby in sight. Rather than put me on the same medication that failed the first time, my doctor opted for a more aggressive approach. It was an injection of a heavy-duty drug that would mimic menopause, therefore shutting down my hormone system that the endometriosis drew from in order to recur.

Another drawback was the cost of the shot, a mere $648 per injection. To add insult to injury, my medical insurance would not cover the full cost of the injection because it was a name brand drug and there was no generic substitute. For six months I paid $250 for each injection which gave me migraines, hot flashes, night sweats, anxiety, and caused intense emotional outbursts. I was miserable physically, emotionally, and financially. Once again I had to set my sights on the first of the year. Another January, another new year with new hope.

After five months of injections and miserable side effects, I began to experience the same symptoms I had become so familiar with. It was apparent that the shots were not working, and once again my life was completely controlled by the pain I felt in everything I did.

I went to my doctor in December, knowing in my heart what he was going to tell me. He explained to me that he had exhausted every medical resource he knew of, and that he couldn't continue to perform surgery on me every year for the rest of my life. It was taking its toll on me physically and emotionally.

I had known in my heart all along that would probably be the end result, yet I still carried some glimmer of hope that perhaps I would be able to have another child. But when I heard the doctor say that very final word "hysterectomy," I resolved that we would never have our little girl. My doctor told me to take three months to ponder and pray about it, and then come back to him with an answer.

During the next two months, I prayed continually for the Lord to help me find peace of mind with the decision I knew I had to make. I needed to know that the Lord had a plan for me, and I had to have faith and accept whatever that plan was and that this surgery was the right thing to do.

I wasn't exactly sure how the Lord was going answer my prayers, but I hoped that a decision this big would warrant some grand vision or overwhelming manifestation such as the heavens parting or a lightning bolt in my kitchen. But as with everything else the Lord touches, my prayers were answered quietly and personally, in a way I never imagined.

One afternoon as I was standing at the stove cooking dinner, the pain raced through me, down my legs, and literally took my breath away and brought me to my knees. As I sat on the floor struggling to work through the pain, these words came to my mind, "Shannon, if you don't have this surgery, the pain won't go away. You'll feel like this for the rest of your life. If you want to feel better, you must do this."

I knew this was true and I was tired of being in pain. I was exhausted. I just wanted to feel good and be happy. I called my doctor the next day and told him I was ready to schedule my hysterectomy.

Just a few days before my surgery, Eric and I had a date night, just mom and son. We went to the mall for the evening and took turns choosing a store to visit. It was one of those evenings that seemed magical. Eric was on his best behavior and I was feeling as maternal and patient as Harriet Nelson. We had so much fun together. As we left the mall when it closed, we walked hand in hand to the car. I turned to my nine-year-old son and said, "Eric, you are the best kid in the whole world. I could never ask for a better son."

He looked up at me with his sparkling blue eyes and said, "And you're the best mom in the world. I could never ask for a better mom." I gazed up at the beautiful night sky and the stars twinkling above. I felt an overwhelming peace enter my body, starting at the top of my head and running to my feet as though warm molasses was filling my body. I heard these words as clear as a bell, "Shannon, he is your blessing. He will fill you with joy and happiness and fulfill you as a woman and mother." I was completely at peace. I knew what I had to do and the peace in my soul told me I was ready.

On February 12, 1999, I had a hysterectomy at the age of thirty-six.

After eight weeks of recuperating physically and emotionally, my life came back into focus and I was overwhelmed by how wonderful I felt. I hadn't realized how good I could feel because I had felt awful for so many years. I had my life back and I loved it. I was able to live my days with a smile on my face and peace in my heart. Tim loved having his wife back, and I loved being there for my family again, able to take care of them instead of them taking care of me. But even in my happiness, my heart continued to echo the chorus of a little girl who was meant to be.

In the year following my hysterectomy, Tim and I looked into several adoption agencies, both domestic and foreign. None seemed right to us. They were too expensive, we were too old, or the waiting list was too long. There was always something that wasn't right about each one. At one point we were close to adopting an eleven-year-old boy through the Department of Social and Health Services. But after months of preparing for him, the social worker placed him with another family. We loved him dearly and were very disappointed that he was not going to be part of our family.

The spring of 2000 started just like the previous three springs had. I was in pain. I didn't understand why I was experiencing it again because I thought my hysterectomy had taken care of all that. Another visit with my doctor revealed that I most likely had scar tissue or a cyst on my right ovary, which was causing the pain.

When I heard my doctor say the word "surgery," I fell into a tunnel of discouragement. I had gone through three surgeries in the last three years, and I didn't think I had the strength to endure a fourth. The only choice I had was to lean on my faith that the Lord would see me through whatever I had to endure. I memorized the scripture in Proverbs 3:5-6: *"Trust in the Lord with all thine heart and lean not unto thine own understanding. In all thy ways acknowledge Him, and he shall direct thy paths."* That verse became the strength that guided me through each day.

On March 10, 2000, I proceeded again with the well-known surgery ritual. My recovery was extremely difficult because for the first time the doctor had to actually make an incision in my abdomen. In addition to removing my right ovary, the doctor also removed my appendix.

Both my physical and emotional recoveries were a challenge. I didn't know how much more I could take. It had been six years since we started our journey to have another child. We had nothing to show except a lot of medical bills, physical and emotional scars, and exhaustion from a long roller coaster ride of emotions.

During the week following my surgery, my best friend of 10 years, Chris, called and invited me to go to a meeting with her about Chinese adoption. Her invitation sparked my curiosity. We had never explored Chinese adoption. We didn't even realize that Chinese children were available for adoption.

The meeting was held at a local public library. The assistant director of Great Wall China Adoption came from Texas to talk about the precious children in China who were available for adoption. I learned about China's one-child policy, the Chinese people's desire for male babies, and the hundreds of thousands of little girls who were abandoned as a result. As I watched the videos and looked at the literature in front of me, I was moved so deeply that tears streamed down my face. At that moment I knew beyond a shadow of a doubt that our little girl was alive and waiting for us in China. It was a burning knowledge that filled my body.

I cried all the way home. Never before had I felt so close to my Heavenly Father and so driven by a force that seemed to consume me. When I arrived home, I recounted the entire evening to Tim. Adrenalin surged through my body and I talked so fast I was sure he couldn't capture everything I was saying. Tim felt the spirit that I brought back with me from the meeting and we knew this was what God had in store for us. We both knew in our hearts that our daughter was in China.

We had decided long before Eric was born that if we had a little girl, she would be named Marlee. The name that had been tucked away in our hearts for so many years was brought to life with this new knowledge of our Chinese daughter. Marlee Turner was now a reality.

We discovered that when something is meant to be, the Lord touches every part of it. Everything that happened to us from that point on was truly a miracle.

Shortly after we made the decision to go forward with the adoption, Tim went out of town on a business trip. He called me one night from his hotel, excited to tell me what had happened to him. He had gone shopping for the evening and stopped to have dinner at a Chinese restaurant at the mall. After his dinner, he curiously opened his fortune cookie. It read, "YOUR ABILITY TO LOVE WILL HELP A CHILD IN NEED."

THE PAPER CHASE

The paperwork involved in a foreign adoption is overwhelming. It is fondly referred to as "the paper chase" among adoptive families. When we received the adoption instruction packet in the mail from Great Wall China Adoption, I sat down and read it from cover to cover. The procedure seemed overwhelming; I cried as I held the instructions in my lap. How could I ever do all this? It seemed too complicated. After reading through the packet again several times, I came to the conclusion that I would approach it the same way a person would eat an elephant: one bite at a time.

The first step of the paper chase was to submit an application, known as I6OOA, to the Immigration and Naturalization Services (INS), an agency that has to give permission before a foreign adoption can take place. I had heard horror stories about INS from other adoptive parents about how difficult they were to deal with and how slowly their process ran.

My experience with INS started out as frustrating as I had expected. I arrived at the local office that was only five blocks from our home and was told by the employee there that they didn't process adoption applications at that office. I would have to travel 90 miles to the Yakima, Washington office to submit my application.

The employee in Richland wasn't exactly on the top of the candidate list for Mr. Congeniality. I was quite discouraged with how mechanical and insensitive he was toward me. I understood that he couldn't change the policy, but he could have been more personable. I turned away from the office rather discouraged, took the day off work, and Chris and I set out for a road trip to Yakima.

The INS worker in Yakima was very nice, contrary to what I had previously experienced in Richland. I asked her how long it would take to get an appointment to be fingerprinted for our background check and her reply was four to six weeks.

She then stepped away from the counter, came back a few moments later, and asked if I could be fingerprinted right then. I was more than happy to get one more thing checked off my to-do list that day. I didn't even have time to sit down in the waiting area before a man came out and called my name.

After I had been fingerprinted for the criminal background check, the very nice gentleman handed me a form. He explained that the form was for my husband

and Tim could just take it to the Richland INS office and be fingerprinted any time without an appointment. I couldn't believe how easy they were making it for us.

Tim went to the INS office near our home the following week and was fingerprinted. The prints were sent to the FBI, cleared, and the results sent back to INS the very same day. What should have taken us two to three months, took less than two weeks.

Our next step was to find a social worker to do our home study. Much to our surprise, it was quite a challenge to find someone willing to do a foreign adoption home study. Every agency we contacted turned us down. When they heard the words "foreign adoption" they acted as if we were asking them to walk on the moon. After many phone calls and rejections, we became quite discouraged.

One day as I was working in my office, the name "LDS Social Services" suddenly popped into my head. It was an obvious resource since I am a member of the Church of Jesus Christ of Latter-Day Saints. I smiled at myself for not thinking of it sooner. I immediately telephoned the local office and explained to a very nice gentleman what we needed.

The kind man explained to me that they did indeed have a social worker that did home studies, but they were for adoptions handled through their agency. I must have sighed very loudly because he paused, then added, "But he is also licensed to do them independently. I'll give him your message and have him return your call." I didn't get my hopes up because of all the previous rejections. But just a few days later, Pat Cabbage returned my call and said that he would be happy to do our home study.

On May 11th, Pat Cabbage came to our home for a very in-depth three-hour interview with our family. He was kind and loving and we felt as if we had known him forever. We shared with him our history and our knowledge that there was a little girl who was meant to be in our family. He had the most loving, sensitive demeanor and we could feel his empathy toward us.

As Mr. Cabbage was getting ready to leave, he asked us if we had any questions about the home study. We hadn't yet discussed the cost, so I apprehensively inquired about the financial arrangements. He pondered for a moment, then quoted us a price well below what we had expected. Tim and I looked at each other in surprise. I asked Mr. Cabbage if that was going to be enough to cover his time and effort because we knew how much work was involved in completing a home study. He paused, put down his pen, leaned across the table and said, "I need to tell you a story."

He looked at us with a fervent stare as if he was about to tell us the secrets of the universe. He settled into his chair and smiled. "I am very surprised to be sitting here in your home doing this home study. I don't normally do foreign adoptions. I have turned down foreign adoption home studies for years. I tell people that I don't do them. It's not like I need the work, because there's plenty to keep me busy. I have done over 1,000 home studies in my 25-year career."

He paused for a moment and I saw a sparkle in his eyes. He smiled and continued, "But my boss came to me with your message and said, 'Pat, I think you need to do this.' I told him that I don't do foreign adoptions and he said, 'I know, but I feel in my heart that you need to do this one.'"

There was silence around our dining room table, and then he continued on with his story. "So here I am. I'm doing this home study to help you get your little girl, not to make money. There are more important things in life than making money."

I was speechless. The tears welled up in my eyes as I reached across the table and put my hands on his. We knew that the Lord had directed us to him.

* * * *

I told Tim that I wanted to start a scrapbook for our daughter so when she was older she could see the things we did in order to adopt her. I dabbled in scrapbooking for a few years and considered it one of my fortes. I was scheduled to attend a scrapbook class the weekend following our home study.

Throughout the class they drew door prizes, with a grand prize at the end of the day. I was surprised to hear my name called as the winner and was presented with a beautiful red scrapbook album. It was the exact scrapbook that I wanted to start for our daughter. Once again, this small little sign confirmed to me that we were doing the right thing.

Throughout our paper chase we were also preparing our daughter's bedroom. We purchased a new bed, mattress set, bedding, and little girl accessories. Choosing a theme, however, was a difficult decision. I had two pictures depicting Jesus with lambs that I wanted to be the focus of her bedroom. I finally decided on lambs and hearts for the theme of her room. The hearts would represent love...our love for her, our love for each other, and Jesus' love for all of us. The lambs would represent our daughter as a child and all of us as children of God. So I set out collecting every lamb, sheep, and heart I could find.

In July, Tim and I went to Seattle for our 14th wedding anniversary. It was there I found out that I had been inspired to choose the theme of our daughter's room. While shopping downtown, we discovered an enchanting store where I found a set of Chinese character rubber stamps. It was just what I was looking for to make Marlee's adoption announcements.

That night I got into bed and started to read the booklet that came with the set of stamps. I curiously turned the pages and found the character "Mei" that means BEAUTY. As I read the definition, I felt that incredibly warm spirit come over me that I had felt so many times before.

"From a Western perspective, the Chinese character for Mei defines beauty in a surprising way. It combines an ancient pictograph, the head of a horned sheep, with the character for big or conceited—a person with arms outstretched. In the Chinese tradition, the sheep is considered the gentlest and most harmonious of animals. It strives for nothing, and its needs are modest and easily satisfied. The character for beauty suggests that people who bear themselves without conceitedness, going gently through life like a sheep and never striving against the order of things, are truly beautiful."[1]

Little did I know when I chose sheep as the theme for her room that the sheep had such significance in the

Chinese culture. I knew that, once again, I had been inspired.

Our dossier, the compilation of papers that was to be sent to China, was finally completed and sent to Great Wall China Adoption on July 21, 2000. When I took it to the post office, the scale tipped out at 2½ pounds. A mere $17.00 in postage later, it was off to Texas!

I had a hard time releasing it into the hands of the postal worker. I explained to her that the package contained four months of paperwork: seventeen different documents, certifications from the Secretary of State, and authentications from the Consulate General of China. It also represented almost $6,000 in costs to obtain all that paperwork. The very kind postal worker assured me it was in good hands as she tossed it in a bin and I watched it disappear into a sea of hundreds of other packages.

The U.S. Postal Service prevailed and Great Wall China Adoption received our dossier the next day. They double-checked all our papers for us and sent it off to China the same week. It was registered with the Chinese Center of Adoption Affairs on August 1, 2000.

Having our dossier in China was a huge weight off our shoulders. The hard work was over and now all we had to do was sit back and wait. We quickly discovered that the hardest work had just begun.

CHALLENGES

Before we started the adoption process, we came up with a financial plan to meet the expenses of the adoption. Through several different resources, we were able to come up with the first portion of money to cover the dossier costs.

I sold my 1976 Triumph Spitfire that I purchased when I was 19 years old. It was hard to see my first car go, but priorities change between age 19 and 36. I didn't care anymore about being a "hot chick" riding in a convertible or hearing my friends say, "What a great car!" We were also able to borrow against a Tax Sheltered Annuity that we had started eleven years before.

In addition, I started a second job as a kitchen consultant doing cooking shows in the evenings after I got off work. I left for work at 7:30 each morning and didn't get home until after 10:00 p.m. on the nights I had shows. It was exhausting, but I knew it was just for a few months. The long hours were softened by the fact that there was a goal in sight. I prayed that this venture would be successful and would help us meet the financial obligations of the adoption.

We knew that when it came time to travel, however, we would need help with the last half of the expenses. We still had to pay for my travel to China, hotels for two weeks, a $3,000 required donation to the orphanage, gifts and medical supplies for the other children in the orphanage, our daughter's visa, passport, doctor's exam, adoption papers, and all the other miscellaneous expenses in China.

Back in the initial stages of our adoption planning, we spoke to our mortgage company and asked them if we could refinance our second mortgage in November to cover the rest of our adoption costs. They said that it wouldn't be a problem and to give them a call in the fall when we needed it.

As fall approached, we called the mortgage company to touch base and get the paperwork going. They informed us they no longer had the program previously discussed and they could not help us. Panic consumed us as we called every lending and mortgage company we could find to see what they could offer.

We quickly found out that refinancing our mortgage was not an option. Most mortgage companies would only finance 90% of the value of a home. Unfortunately, the value of our home had decreased since it was last appraised. Because of the number of new housing developments in our area, the government homes like ours, all about 60 years old, had taken a drastic hit in market value. Because of this, the balance of our mortgage exceeded the 90% that could be financed.

I tried banks, credit unions, everyone I could think of. After several weeks of frustration from being turned down for one reason or another, I was referred to a bank that had a 125% mortgage program. I explained everything to a very nice lady and she said that it sounded like they'd be able to help us. I couldn't believe my ears! She said she'd call me the next day and we'd get everything started.

The next day came and I didn't receive a phone call as promised, so I called the office again. The woman I had spoken to previously explained that she'd found a problem. Our income was fine, our debt ratio was fine, but our credit rating had dropped below their minimum requirement. I told her I didn't understand how that could be possible. I had received a copy of our credit report just three months before and nothing should have changed.

She explained to me that every time a company inquired about a person's credit rating, it lowered the person's credit score. With all the inquiries into our credit history lately, it had lowered our credit rating so much that we had no chance of getting a loan from anyone.

Little did we know that our frantic attempts during the past month to find someone to help us was actually sabotaging our chances even more. If only we had called this company first! We were devastated, depressed, and ready to throw in the towel. Our last hope had failed. We felt like the dream of our little girl was vanishing before our eyes. I tried to imagine how we were going to tell our son that his little sister wasn't going to be a reality after all.

The following day on the way home from an evening activity, I was pondering all of the recent events in my mind. I was thinking about our little girl and pictured her asleep in her bed in the orphanage. The tears came to my eyes as I imagined never being able to hold her, kiss her cheeks, and give her a life of love and family. My heart broke as I imagined her life in an orphanage with no hope of a future.

The feeling of desperation overwhelmed me and I had to find something to distract me or else I was going to fall apart. I turned on the car radio to hear my favorite nighttime dedication show. The host of the show happened to be talking about special people who were far away, and the thought suddenly came to me that I should dedicate a song to our little girl.

When I arrived home I logged on to their website and sent a dedication to go out to our daughter who lived in an orphanage in China. I asked them to play the song, "Somewhere Out There" and explained our story very briefly. I had no idea when the song would be played, but I was comfortable with just dedicating the song and knowing it would eventually be aired.

As I logged off the computer, I suddenly remembered that I had to take a book over to a friend's house. Although it was late, she needed it the next day. It was almost 10:00 p.m. by the time I arrived at her house. I walked up to her door, rang the doorbell, and stood waiting for the door to open. Just then I noticed something in front of me. I blinked my tired eyes to focus on a beautiful little ladybug clinging to the screen door. The tears welled up in my eyes and I knew this little ladybug was a sign.

I had learned months earlier that the ladybug was a symbol of good luck for people adopting children from China. Throughout the recent history of Chinese adoptions, families who were adopting children associated the sightings of ladybugs with good news. Many stories circulated about these little bugs and the good news they carried with them. My story was no different; I knew this little bug was telling me something. I moved in closer to somehow hear its whispers of inspiration. In my heart it spoke to me and assured me that everything would work out. I must rely on my faith.

The next morning I went about my daily routine. I arrived in my office, put my purse away and turned on my computer and radio, just like I did every morning. I sat down at my desk as a commercial finished on the radio and a new song started. As I heard the introduction, I felt a warm tingle all through my body. The song "Somewhere Out There" filled my office. I sat motionless and listened to the inspiring words. *"Somewhere out there, someone's saying a prayer, that we'll find one another, in that big somewhere out there."*[2]

When the song ended I turned off the radio and sat in silence. For the first time I realized that not only was I yearning and praying for my daughter, but our little girl was also carrying a prayer in her heart that her mommy and daddy would soon come rescue her from her meager surroundings. I envisioned my sweet little girl saying her prayers and asking God for a family.

I wiped away the tears, heaved a huge sigh of desperation, and then turned my attention to my computer to begin working. I opened my e-mail and saw my "daily inspiration" from the list that I subscribed to. The title was "Trials in Life." It was a quote from Orson F. Whitney:

> *"No pain that we suffer, no trial that we experience is wasted. It ministers to our education, to the development of such qualities as patience, faith, fortitude and humility. All*

that we suffer and all that we endure, especially when we endure it patiently, builds up our characters, purifies our hearts, expands our souls, and makes us more tender and charitable, more worthy to be called children of God. It is through sorrow and suffering, toil and tribulation, that we gain the education that we come here to acquire". [3]

This was the inspiration I needed at the exact time I needed it. I knew this was my sign to not give up; I had to press forward with strength and faith. I had a sure knowledge that our little girl was meant to be in our family. I just wished that I knew how it was going to happen.

WORK AND PRAYER

Throughout my life I had heard the saying, "Pray as if it all depends on God, then work as if it all depends on you." The days were passing by all too quickly, and we were looking at the calendar with a lot of anxiety. It was the end of September already, and we were just a few weeks away from receiving our referral, the official notification from the Chinese Center of Adoption Affairs of our daughter's identity.

Just a few short weeks after that, we would receive my travel arrangements. And the grim reality of it all was that the money we had been assured would be there for us wasn't there after all. We had to raise $10,000 and we had three months in which to do it. I was doing as many as three kitchen shows a week, but the money just wasn't as lucrative as I had anticipated it would be. Tim and I were feeling the weight of the task ahead of us and the pressure of the clock ticking away.

One day at work, as I was talking to a friend who was an attorney, I asked him about the legalities of fund-raising. I confided in him our situation and offered various ideas about fund-raising. He told me that if he were in my situation, he would put an ad in the local paper asking for donations. I explained to him that I felt like it was begging, but he said he thought that we would get a good response. He believed people would look at it as a good and noble thing that we were doing and want to help. I contemplated his suggestion as I was driving back to my office.

I decided to stop by my favorite bagel shop to wallow my sorrows in carbohydrates and cream cheese. Two of my co-workers from the police department were also there enjoying a morning bagel. One of the officers asked me how the adoption was going, and I told him about the recent financial setback. He told me that he was the president of his police association and asked me to write him a letter explaining our financial requirements of the adoption. He would take the letter to his association and see if they could make a donation.

The other officer then joined in and said that he was the treasurer of his association and asked me to do the same for him. They assured me that they had faith that everything would work out for us. I told him that I also knew it would, but I just didn't know how.

My co-workers' optimism and support gave me an idea. There were a lot of police associations around the Tri-Cities, and I had known many of those officers for 19 years or more. Why not go to each association with the same letter? That night I drafted a letter explaining our adoption and asking for any assistance they might be able to give us.

Then my thoughts went beyond just law enforcement. I thought about all the professional contacts I had made throughout my years working in the criminal justice system. I sat down and made a list of people I could send letters to. When I was finished, I had listed 105 names.

I was starting to feel somewhat hopeful. I kept thinking about how the Lord has challenged us to bear one another's burdens. If ever there was a time we needed some help, it was now. I prayed with all my might that the people would be touched and willing to help. As difficult as it was to humble ourselves and ask for help, we knew that was our only choice.

The next day on my lunch hour I went to a local credit union and asked if I could open up a donation account. One of the tellers there had been following our adoption process since the onset and she was more than happy to help me. We named the account, "Marlee's Orphanage Fund."

Over the next three days I wrote, addressed and mailed out all 105 letters. Tim and I decided that we would wait for a month and see what we could bring in from our letters. If we still needed more assistance, we would consider putting an ad in the paper. I wanted to hold off for as long as possible before publicly announcing to 180,000 people that we were desperate.

THE YARD SALE

Since mid-summer I had been planning an "adoption yard sale." I sent out flyers to friends, co-workers and church members asking for donated items for the yard sale. I planned to have the yard sale on September 29th and 30th. For the entire month of September we had people bringing donated items to our house in an overwhelming show of support. Our basement and driveway were packed! In the evenings after work when I didn't have kitchen shows, I would go through all the donated items to price them, all the while praying that the yard sale would be a success.

The weather in September was absolutely gorgeous. The days were record setting warm, but the crisp smell of autumn was in the air. The week of the yard sale arrived, and I was busily getting things in order.

As I was preparing dinner one evening, I was listening to the news on television. The forecast for the week was sunny and beautiful...until the weekend. On Friday they predicted the weather would be windy and cloudy, then on Saturday the forecast was RAIN! I couldn't believe it! It had been sunny for the entire month. How dare it rain on my yard sale, the one I had worked my head off for! But I resolved there was nothing I could do but to forge ahead and hope that the "weather guessers," as my father called them, would be wrong.

As with everything else in my life, Murphy's Law prevailed. The weather forecast was right on the nail. I got up at 4:30 on Friday morning and started setting up for the yard sale. The weather was a little unstable, but nothing that would stand in my way! By 7:30 a.m. I had everything ready to go, and the customers started to roll in.

One of my first customers was my friend, Gretchen, who stopped by simply to leave us a donation. She gave me a hug and wished us luck in our efforts. Her words of encouragement set the tone, as I was steadily busy all morning.

Many customers commented that they had never seen so many people at a yard sale. When I listed it in the paper, I titled it "Adoption Yard Sale." Several people asked about the adoption and offered words of encouragement. Many also said, "Keep the change," and cited that it was for a good cause. I had printed up cards explaining that we were earning money for our adoption expenses and handed them out to each person who purchased something.

One gentleman bought an air compressor that a friend of ours had donated. About an hour later, he returned to tell me that the compressor worked very well. He had read the card about the adoption and wanted to come back and give us more money to help with the costs.

Everything was going well until about noon when the wind kicked into high gear. Things started blowing all over the yard, and many glass items fell over and were broken. The clouds were dark and dirty and I knew it wasn't going to get any better, so I started to put things away. With the help of my brother and sister-in-law, we had everything cleaned up by about 3:00 p.m. I finally sat down to tally our profit for the day and it came to just under $500. I was very pleased.

I was so tired that every part of me ached. I cringed at the thought of having to do it all over again the next day. I went to bed that night secretly hoping it would rain as the forecasters had predicted, but then felt guilty for feeling that way.

The alarm went off at 4:30 a.m. just as it had the day before. I went outside to find the wind howling, dark clouds looming, and the smell of rain in the air. It was definitely not yard sale weather. I could tell there was no chance of it clearing any time soon.

I put up a big sign in our front window that said, "Bad weather, no yard sale" and went back to bed, somewhat relieved. I soon heard the rain tapping on the windows and the screech of the wind. As I listened to the rain, discouraged about the second half of my yard sale, I was reminded in my thoughts that when the Lord closes one door, He opens another.

I decided to go out and do errands that morning while Tim and Eric stayed home. Shortly after I had left home, there was a knock at our door. Tim opened it to meet a very nice lady named Sara. She said she had seen our ad for the yard sale in the paper and wanted to come by and make a donation. She handed Tim a check for $20 and explained that they had adopted their two-year-old daughter from China about six months previously. She also said she would be happy to answer any questions we might have and offer support. Tim briefly explained our financial frustrations. Sara said that she firmly believed there were people out there who would be willing to help.

Shortly after the visit from Sara, there was another knock at the door. It was our friend, Pam, who came to give us a donation from their family. She handed Tim $100 in cash and wished us luck.

That night the windows of heaven opened up and poured out rain like I had never seen before. Even though it had rained on our yard sale, I saw these raindrops as an indication of the outpouring of love and generosity from our friends, as well as total strangers. I decided to gather my energy once again and set my sights on the next Saturday to try the yard sale once again.

The next morning was beautiful, just like the song about our favorite determined spider, "Out came the sun and dried up all the rain." I pondered the fact that the only two days the weather had been bad were the two days of my yard sale. Was it just coincidence or was the adversary trying to prevent us from attaining our goal of adopting our little girl?

I had felt for a very long time that the future Marlee Turner had great things in store for her; that she was going to take the world by storm. I had heard many times throughout my life that great things are often met by opposition. I wondered if that was the case with the storm over the weekend. But whatever the reason for the weather, I wasn't going to let a little wind and rain get me down. I had recently heard Gordon B. Hinckley say about great accomplishments, "It shows you what you can get done if you set an objective and work your head off." [4]

As we walked into church Sunday morning, we were greeted by a long-time friend. I had known him since I was a child and Tim had recently worked very closely with him at church. He walked directly to us and said that he had received our letter in the mail. He pulled out his checkbook and wrote us a check. As he handed it to me, I put my arms around his neck and gave him a big hug. He responded by quietly saying, "Just save me a hug from your sweet little Chinese daughter." Tim and I were overwhelmed by his generosity.

During the course of the day, several people asked about the success of the yard sale. When I told them I was going to do it again the following Saturday because of the inclement weather, many people said they had things they still wanted to donate. At first I cringed at the thought of going through more stuff to price, but then I realized it was a blessing. Our friends were there to help ease our burden, one way or another.

I spent the next week getting ready to do the yard sale all over again. Tim and Eric left town on Friday, so I was on my own for the second go-around. I worked hard

Friday night getting everything set up so I wouldn't have to get up at 4:00 a.m. again. I was busily carrying boxes here and there when I tripped over a board that was lying in the driveway. I fell, dropped the box, and twisted my ankle and my back. I picked myself up and immediately wondered if I had broken my ankle. But then Tim's famous words to his high school girls' volleyball team came to mind, "The best ones play hurt." I brushed myself off and limped around trying to finish getting things set up.

Finally, around 10:00 p.m., I had finished and was completely exhausted. I covered all the tables with tarps and started getting ready for bed. I suddenly remembered that I hadn't fed the dogs their dinner, so I took a bowl of food out to their kennel. As I bent down to fill their dish, our two-year-old German shepherd, Luca, came running to greet me. Our heads met at a high rate of speed, and the impact almost knocked me out. My head was spinning and I thought I was going to faint. I made my way to the house, sat down on the front porch, and started to cry. I cried for an hour. I couldn't stop. I was exhausted and frustrated. Could anything else possibly go wrong? The only thing I could do was cry.

My sweet sister-in-law, Chris, came to my rescue the next morning. She knew Tim was gone and called to see if I needed help with the yard sale. Help was certainly an understatement. I needed strength, mental stamina, inspiration, and a new ankle. She was my saving angel that morning. She did a lot of the physical running around for me while I sat at the money table with my ankle propped up. Not only did she help me physically, but emotionally as well. She lifted my spirits and eased my burden.

When we tallied up the sales from the day, it came to $325, for a grand total of $825 for both days. Chris left at noon to go to her son's soccer game and I handled the rest of the sale on my own. Finally at 1:30 I started to clean up for the last time.

A friend from church came over and took a load to the dump for me. I piled the rest of the boxes in the driveway to take to a charity. I cleaned up our driveway until 5:30 that night, still hobbling around on my sore ankle. I still had so much stuff left over, but there was no way on God's beautiful green earth that I was going to do another day of yard sale.

That evening I anxiously dove into the longest, richest bubble bath I had ever taken. I felt like a huge weight was lifted off my shoulders to be finished with the yard sale. I swore then and there I would never do another yard sale again in my life! I also realized that the words "yard" and "sale" were both four-letter words. My mother taught me never to use four-letter words!

The yard sale was over, but I couldn't relax for long. My next goal was to book as many kitchen shows as possible. I did seven kitchen shows in October, and at each show there were three or four people who also wanted to have a show. Before I knew it, I had booked thirteen shows for November. I had no idea how I was going to find the time or energy to do it. This was what I'd been praying for, so I knew I had to summon the energy from somewhere to get the job done.

My life consisted of working 40 hours a week at the Police Department, doing kitchen shows, running to and from Tim's volleyball games and Eric's Cub Scouts, and doing the ever-present housework. The only time I sat down was to sleep. I literally ran from one thing to the next. I started to get very worried about myself and wondered if I was on the verge of a breakdown.

I'm sure that the stress of my busy life showed on my weary face, because many people cautioned me and said that I was doing too much and needed to slow down. My response to them was, "I can't slow down. I have to do my part. If I want to be blessed, I have to pull my share of the weight. When I'm on the plane to China, then I'll relax. Until then, I will work with all my might to make this dream come true."

THE WALL

November came and I continued to run at full speed. I was up to three or four kitchen shows each week. Tim's volleyball team that he coached had advanced to post-season play. I was starting to feel a little run down and was having episodes of dizziness accompanied by nausea. I dismissed it as being related to fatigue and kept on with my busy schedule.

The weekend of November 10th was the state volleyball tournament in Yakima, Washington. Mid-way through the first day of play, I started feeling very sick. The dizziness and nausea got worse, and I actually considered going to the hospital. But instead, I continued to watch the games, feeling worse as the weekend went on.

The tournament finished, and we came home from Yakima on Saturday night. I went straight to bed and spent the rest of the weekend there.

I forced myself to crawl into work on Monday morning and was miserable all day. That evening I spent getting ready for the four kitchen shows I had scheduled that week. I fell into bed, wondering how I was ever going to find the energy to do everything that was ahead of me that week.

Tuesday morning I struggled to get ready for work, so dizzy I could hardly stand up. I made it to work and only lasted two hours before I knew I had to go home. The dizziness and nausea were so bad I couldn't focus on anything. I slept all day, then got up in the early evening to get ready to go to my show that night.

The whole evening I struggled to keep my composure and be professional. My head was spinning, and I felt like I was going to faint. I heard the words coming out of my mouth, but had no idea what I was saying. I'm not sure how I made it through the night, especially driving twenty-five miles to and from Benton City, but I finished my evening with success.

Getting out of bed the next morning was not a physical option for me. Just turning my head from side to side on my pillow made the room spin around. I slept until noon and then dragged myself to work, only to have to leave after just a few hours.

I finally decided it was time to call the doctor. Luckily, I was able to get an appointment for the following morning. I called my hostess for the kitchen show that night to see if we could postpone her show, but she had many people confirmed and was anxiously awaiting her party. I found the rest of the strength that was left inside my body and used it to do her show that night.

I walked into my doctor's office on Thursday morning expecting to walk out with an antibiotic that would have me back on my feet in just a couple days. My doctor looked in my ears, eyes, throat, and did a series of intriguing tests. Then she informed me that she believed I had a condition called Labyrinthitis, a viral disease that affects the working relationship between the inner ears, eyes and limbs.

My doctor explained that there was good news and bad news associated with that diagnosis. The good news was that she was going to give me some motion sickness medication that would help me be more comfortable. Unfortunately, it would make me very drowsy. The other bad news was that there was nothing she could do to make the Labyrinthitis go away. She said it would just have to run its course and could take up to six weeks for that to happen.

Then, to add insult to injury, she told me that I would not be able to go back to work until the following week. I was devastated. I told her that I didn't have time to be sick, that I had too many things to do. She smiled empathetically and said, "Well, I'm sorry." My doctor wrote me a note and faxed it to my sergeant at the police department explaining why I wouldn't be back to work for a while. My precious sick time that I had been saving to use for my trip to China was vanishing before my eyes! To coin a phrase from my father, I walked out of the office "madder than a wet hen."

I spent the afternoon fretting about my situation and wondering how on earth I was going to make it through the holiday season constantly feeling like I had just stepped off a carnival ride. To make matters worse, I had a kitchen show that night, and the hostess was expecting twenty people. I prayed with all my might that I would somehow have the strength to get through it. I didn't dare take the medication the doctor had given me, for fear it would knock me out and I wouldn't be able to do my show. Fortunately, my dear friend, Kerrilynn, was the hostess, and she helped me get everything ready.

I know that power from heaven assisted me that night. As the guests arrived, the dizziness went away and I felt better than I had in weeks. I did the show with great ease and it was a huge success. When all the orders were in, it turned out to be my biggest show so far. I credited Kerri for the success of the show. She went above and beyond her responsibilities as a hostess to be sure that the party was a success for me. That night I thanked the Lord for good friends like Kerri who were there to help me through the hard times.

The next day I sat and contemplated the tasks ahead of me in the upcoming weeks. I had seven kitchen shows. I needed to prepare two hundred invitations for a church function. Then there was Thanksgiving and, oh yes, my Christmas Open House for my kitchen hostesses and customers. I also had four commitments to play my cello for Christmas functions. All that was sprinkled with the fact that my head was spinning around like a top all the time. It was truly going to take strength beyond what I had inside me to do it all.

BLESSINGS FROM HEAVEN

Friends are the flowers in the garden of life. I was having a particularly frustrating day when my dear friend, Chris, called. She had recently moved to the other side of the state in the Seattle area. It was hard having her so far away, as she had been my rock of strength for over 10 years. I welcomed her call like a big glass of lemonade in the Sahara Desert.

Chris had just returned from visiting her mother in Olympia. There she had met a co-worker of her mother's who had also adopted a little girl from China. The woman mentioned to Chris that she hadn't yet done the paperwork to have her daughter's name changed. Chris, having helped a friend do this four times previously, said she was familiar with the steps it took to do so and offered to help her.

The woman was overjoyed and asked her how much she could pay her to do it. Chris told her about our family and our frantic attempts to earn money. Chris then handed her one of the donation cards that I had made up and asked her to just send a contribution to Marlee's Orphanage Fund instead of paying her.

The woman read the card and then told Chris that she wanted to share this with her reunion group. She pointed to a picture on the wall of many women with Chinese little girls. It was a group of women that she had traveled with to China. She said that she thought her reunion group would like to help.

With the telephone receiver to my ear, the words of hope and generosity were like a beacon in the night to me. I hung up the phone, determined that I wouldn't let a little dizziness bring me down. Once again I repeated to myself, "Every time God closes a door, He opens another one." The doors were just starting to open, but I had no idea just how many doors there would be.

On Wednesday, November 22, the day before Thanksgiving, Tim and Eric came home early from school in preparation for the holiday. Tim called me at work to tell me he had retrieved the mail from the mailbox and found an envelope that had only our names on it. Inside was a card that contained a typed note. It read:

Dear Shannon and Tim,

Do you know how sometimes we feel the love of our Heavenly Father through others? I have felt this incredible love through the generosity of others several times. It has been an incredible experience and blessing to me and strengthened my testimony greatly. Now, because of my circumstances, I get to be a deliverer of His love to you! This is to help you on your quest to get your daughter. I know you feel the support and sustaining love of our Father, and here is a bit more evidence. The Lord is overseeing this whole process, excited for what you are learning...the patience, the faith, the perseverance, the tenacity. All the God-like qualities you are developing as you pursue your family. Please know that you are loved. I support you with all my heart, and a bit of my pocket book! It's so great, what you are doing.

Love,

A Friend

Along with the note there was a cashier's check in the amount of $500. Tim was so overwhelmed by the kind words; he could hardly talk as he read them to me. We couldn't believe the generosity of that dear friend.

Initially, I wanted to know who this kind person was. But as I pondered on it more, I was comforted by the fact that the person wanted to remain anonymous. I had been taught that truly selfless acts are done with no expectation of praise, thanks, or reward. If the person had wanted us to know their identity, they would have told us. So I resolved to let them remain an angel with no name, and knew that they would receive their reward in heaven for their kind, generous gift to us.

Thanksgiving weekend was filled with family, food, and friends. The rumor running amidst the Great Wall China Adoption families on the e-mail group was that there was a group of adoption referrals on the way. We hoped that ours would be in that group of referrals, but we knew it wasn't very likely.

The July expedited referrals hadn't even come in yet, and ours had just missed the July cut-off and was registered on August 1. We were almost certain that ours would be in the next batch that would most likely come at the end of December. Tim, Eric and I were disappointed that we would have to wait a few more weeks, but we resolved that since we had waited so many years for another child, we could wait just a little while longer. Our hearts wanted her now, but our savings account certainly needed a little more time.

During that long weekend of giving thanks, I prayed with all my heart that the people at the Chinese Center of Adoption Affairs would be led to our daughter, the one the Lord had chosen for us, and that she would be kept safe and healthy. When I prayed, I felt calm and comforted. When I wasn't praying, I was stressed, frustrated, and discouraged. So every moment I had, I prayed like I had never prayed before. It was the only thing that gave me peace.

On the morning of November 28, I had barely sat down in my office to start the day when the phone rang. I heard a voice say, "Shannon, how are you today?" It was Jo Anne Bailey, the Washington State representative of Great Wall China Adoption. I didn't think her call was out of the ordinary, because she phoned frequently to see how the adoption was progressing.

She continued her greeting by saying, "I just called to tell you congratulations; you're a mama!" There was a moment of silence. I couldn't believe what I had just heard. Her words echoed in my head. I was so stunned I couldn't even talk. Tears filled my eyes as I struggled to find words. It was as if the intensity of every emotion I had felt for the last eight months was filling my body at once.

I floundered to get a pen in my hand and find a piece of paper to write on. This was the moment I had been waiting for! I was scared and excited at the same time. My heart raced, and I could scarcely breathe as I anticipated Jo Anne's words that would follow.

Her name was Fu Dan, and she was born on October 15, 1997. That made her three years and one month old. At her last doctor's visit on September 19, 2000, she weighed 33 pounds and was 38 inches tall. She had 20 teeth. My hand was shaking as I wrote down this precious information. She lived in the Dandong Child Welfare Institute in the Province of Liaoning in Northern China.

Jo Anne finished by saying that Great Wall would e-mail me a picture of her as soon as they could. I hung up the phone and stared at the information I had just written. I read it over and over. I couldn't believe the day had finally come! This was our daughter. The shaky writing on a small notepad that was already smeared by tears called out to me. "Here I am Mommy. I'm finally here."

After I stopped shaking and crying, I called Tim on the cellular phone. I knew he was in the middle of class, but I thought this justified a special interruption. He answered the phone and I told him that I had exciting news to tell him. He hesitated, and then asked, "Did we get it?"

With my voice quivering and tears still streaming, I responded, "We got it. We got our referral." Tim's voice started to shake as he exclaimed in excitement. We both sniffled through the tears as I repeated the information about our daughter to him. I told him that a picture would be coming soon and I would forward it to him as soon as I received it.

They say that a watched pot never boils. Staring at a computer screen, wishing that little "you've got mail" box would appear, is somewhat the same. I was fixated on my computer for the longest time, and then decided I'd better keep myself busy while I was waiting. I took my tear-stained face around the police station to tell all my co-workers about my exciting news.

I finally returned to my office and started calling family and friends when the e-mail from Great Wall appeared on my computer. I screamed with excitement when I saw it flash on the screen. I sat and stared at the box on the screen and was both excited and scared to open it. I closed my eyes and held my breath, then a quick click of the mouse revealed the picture of our daughter. I melted into the computer screen and stared into the face of the most beautiful little girl in the world. Her sad little eyes looked back at me as if they were saying, "I've been waiting for you."

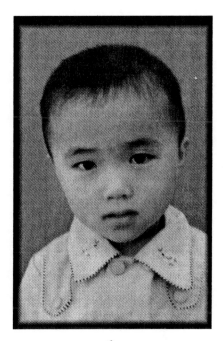

I called Tim once again and told him I was about to send the e-mail. It only took just a few seconds for him to get it, and he opened it as we were talking on the phone. He was quiet for a few moments as he studied her face, then he peacefully said, "She's beautiful."

I printed our daughter's picture and ran around the police station like a crazy woman, waiving her picture in front of everyone's face. I was on an adrenaline rush and spinning around like a whirling dervish. Everyone who crossed my path was attacked by a picture and the question, "Do you want to see my daughter?" Just the words made me cry. I couldn't believe that we finally had a little girl.

That evening after work I stopped and bought a frame to put Marlee's picture in to present to Eric. I also picked up a bake-at-home pizza, which was our idea of a treat, and hurried home. Eric saw me walk in the door and exclaimed, "Oh, pizza!"

Although I wanted to scream in excitement, I tried to casually walk into the kitchen, lay down my things, and turn to meet his eyes. I responded to his exclamation by saying, "Well, I thought that since today was such a special day, we deserved something special."

Eric cocked his head to the side, looked at me with a puzzled look, and then all of a sudden his eyes widened as the light bulb went on. He got a big smile on his face and said, "I think I know why it's a special day! Did we get Marlee's picture?" When I told him that we had, he jumped up and down with excitement. I showed him his little sister's picture and he studied it for a long time. After many different expressions from his face, he finally commented, "So that's her, huh? She's cute."

Eric wondered where in China she was living, so we grabbed our world atlas and discovered that the city of Dandong was located on the border of China and North Korea. We were very surprised by how far north she lived, as most of the orphanages were located in Southern China. But once again, everything about our experience so far was extraordinary, so why should it stop now?

We sat around the dining room table and said a special prayer before dinner. We thanked the Lord for sending us a precious little girl and asked Him to keep her safe until time for me to travel to China and bring her home to be part of our family forever.

CHRISTMAS BLESSINGS

The day following our referral call, Great Wall mailed us three pictures of Marlee along with her medical records. They all indicated she was a beautiful, healthy little girl.

The next several days were filled with tears of joy, telephone calls, and e-mails. All three of us were spinning around with excitement. On Friday, December 1ˢᵗ, I received an e-mail from Leigh Anne, the assistant director of Great Wall China Adoption, with news that was both exciting and alarming.

She explained that they had just received notice from the Chinese Center of Adoption Affairs that procedures had changed for processing travel plans. This new policy would take effect that day and would expedite travel plans, taking as much as four to six weeks off the travel wait. So instead of my plans to leave in mid-February, it was now very likely I would leave in January.

When I heard that news, I was overjoyed at the thought of meeting our daughter sooner. However, there were still about 7,000 reasons why I wasn't prepared, all of them represented by a dollar bill. So far we had raised a little over $3,000 with the profits from my kitchen shows, the yard sale, and individual donations. To our disappointment, the letters I sent out in September didn't generate much of a response. Out of 105 letters, only eight people responded. We had six weeks to find the remaining $7,000.

I didn't have a lot of time to worry that day, because the following day was my open house that I had been planning for months. I had mailed out 175 invitations to all my customers, decorated my house from top to bottom, prepared food galore, and had door prizes and recipes for the guests. I was up until 1:00 a.m. the night before getting everything ready and looking just so.

I rolled out of bed at 6:30 a.m. and starting preparing for my guests. By 10:00 a.m. the punch was sparkling, the food was ready, the table looked great, and Christmas music was playing on the stereo. I was ready.

I anxiously watched as cars passed by, but none of them stopped. Finally, at 11:00 a.m. my first guest arrived. Another hour went by and still nobody came. At 1:00 p.m. another guest came. Just after she left, my mother stopped by and then my sister-in-law. It was 3:00 p.m. and only four guests had come. I was discouraged and frustrated. Then finally at 5:00 another guest and her husband arrived. When they left at 5:30, I started to clean up, assuming I wasn't going to have any more customers.

Just as I started to put things away, there was a knock at the door. My friend, Gretchen, apologized for being so late, but wanted to purchase a few items. When she left at 6:00, the time for the open house was officially over and I had had a total of six customers. I was more than disappointed. I had spent a lot of time, effort, and money to make it successful and it was far from it.

Throughout my life, I kept a firm belief that the Lord will bless a person's efforts and good intentions. Mid-way through the day when I began to realize that my open house was not going to be a success, I tried to hold on to that conviction. I knew that He knew how hard I worked and that I was trying with all my might.

My goal was to profit $250 from my open house, but it looked as if I was going to take a $150 loss instead. It reminded me of the saying, "One step forward, two steps back." I resolved that I would just have to make that money through some other venture.

I think that the intensity of my frustration was so strong, the vibes went to heaven instantly. That afternoon the mailman delivered the answer to my prayers. It was a Christmas card from our friends who lived in Benton City. They wrote a beautiful message about their support and excitement for our new daughter. In addition, they enclosed a check for $270. Tim and I were overwhelmed by their generosity and knew they were an instrument in the Lord's hands to bless us on the road to getting our little girl.

The next day was filled with so much love and gratitude. When we arrived at church, all our friends were excited to share in the happiness of our adoption referral. We showed them pictures of our beautiful new daughter and they showered us with hugs and congratulations in return.

After our church services, we went to an annual choral festival at a local church. It was held each year on the first Sunday in December to start the Christmas season. I had either been in the choir or played my cello with them for many years and loved participating in this multidenominational celebration. This year I was playing my cello to accompany our church choir that was singing in the celebration.

Somehow the carols we sang that night were more meaningful and I sang with more conviction than ever. My heart was so filled with joy for the wonderful gift the Lord had given us. Following that service, we went to our own church for the annual Christmas devotional. The entire day had been filled with the Christmas spirit and I didn't want it to end.

RED THREADS

Monday morning alarm clocks should be banned from society. Even better, Mondays should be banned altogether. I kept hitting the snooze button over and over, then finally our German shepherd, Luca, put her nose to mine and stared me in the face as if to say, "Get your tired body out of bed. You have work to do!" My busy, emotional weekend had caught up with me, and I was exhausted.

I dragged myself into the shower and started thinking about the week ahead of me. I had five days of work, four kitchen shows to close, three shows to do, two music rehearsals, and one performance. I hesitated, smiled, then finished the list by singing comically, "And a partridge in a pear tree."

When I got to work and started up my computer, I had an e-mail waiting for me from Great Wall. It was the final page of our referral we had been waiting for, a letter from the orphanage director that had been translated into English from Chinese.

Throughout our wait for our daughter, I knew in my heart there would be one specific thing about her that would be an indication that she was truly the little girl the Lord had chosen for us. I didn't know what it would be, but I knew that I would know in my heart the minute I heard it. I felt that it would be some type of common bond that she and I would have. The letter confirmed my belief, and I wept as I read it:

"Fu Dan (a girl who can bring you luck), female, was born on October 15, 1997. She was sent to our welfare home

on October 16, 1997. On her arrival, in the parcel wrapped her, a scrip told us that her birth time is 10:40 a.m. On October 15, her check-up showed that her facial features were regular, her limbs were normal and her spirit was good. She was a healthy girl. Her physical and intelligence development were both on target. She has 3 meals and 2 snacks between meals, and 1 nap at noon per day. She has 2 baths per week. She can take care of herself. Her personality was introversive, clever, gentle and quiet. Her receptivity is very good. She can play with other children and communicate with them. She likes dolls."

That was it! Dolls! My little girl liked dolls. The words ran through my body, and I knew that was what I had been waiting to hear. I had been attracted to dolls throughout these last few months, and now I knew why.

I couldn't pass by a doll in the store without stopping and wanting to buy it. I had collected several dolls for her already that were on her bed waiting for her.

Months earlier, I had retrieved my childhood dollhouse from my parents' house and had been working on restoring and updating it for her. I had loved dolls ever since I was little, and now my little girl loved dolls also.

Our family continued to spin around with excitement, but I was spinning a little more than Tim and Eric were. Not because I was happier, but because my world was literally spinning around. The dizziness and nausea were back in full force, and it was worse than it had been before.

After a couple experiences of literally falling down, I decided to call the doctor again. She informed me she was going to send me to an audiologist to have a test done.

She suspected an inner ear condition and wanted to have it verified by a test. I explained to her that my trip to China was quickly approaching, and that I needed to have this condition cleared up before I traveled. I was more than a little concerned, but I put on my happy face that week and did two kitchen shows. They were both quite successful and, more importantly, inspiring.

The first show was for a wonderful lady named Marijke. I felt a common bond with her because she had a biological son who was Eric's age, and she also had three adopted children, including a daughter from Korea. That night I couldn't take my eyes off her adorable daughter, who was nine years old. I couldn't help but picture Marlee at that age. I just wanted to reach out and give her a big hug. I didn't want to freak the poor girl out by clutching her and sobbing uncontrollably, so I just admired her from a distance.

The following evening I did another kitchen show for a lady named Sharon whom I had met back in November. We were introduced by Lisa, who also held a show. Lisa had introduced me to some of the nicest ladies I ever met. They all expressed so much support and interest in our adoption. In fact, three of them wanted to have kitchen shows just to help with the adoption. I was so moved by their friendship and support.

My venture into this business was for moneymaking purposes, but I found that I was making new friends, which was far more valuable than a monthly commission check. One lady offered to give me a coat to take to China. Another offered to give me her daughter's clothes she had outgrown. I was overwhelmed by their sweet generosity. These women were angels on earth, and I will always be grateful to them for their generosity and friendship.

At the beginning of my kitchen shows, I asked the ladies to introduce themselves. We started Sharon's show this way and went around the room meeting each other. It became the turn of a very sweet lady sitting in front of the fireplace. She said, "Hi, my name is Marlee." My eyes bugged out and my jaw dropped.

"Did you say your name is Marlee?" I asked. She looked at me a little shocked, and then verified that her name was, in fact, Marlee. After I got over my shock, I explained to the ladies that the purpose of my job as a kitchen consultant was to earn money for the adoption of our daughter, who we planned to name Marlee.

The room fell silent as all the ladies gasped in unison! Marlee had a surprised look on her face. After a moment of silence, she put her hand to her chest, paused, and said, "I was adopted."

There is a Chinese belief that when a child is born, an invisible red thread stretches out and connects that child with everyone who will be influential in his or her life. The thread may stretch and bend, but it will never break. Meeting Marlee Middleton, who was also adopted, was an apparent red thread. In some way I felt closer to my daughter by meeting this Marlee.

MIRACLES OF THE SEASON

As the days passed during the Christmas season, the miracles of love continued to pour out from heaven. One afternoon as I was sitting in my office, I received a phone call from a gentleman who was a reporter with the Tri-City Herald, our local newspaper. He explained that he had heard that we were adopting a little girl from China and wanted to offer his assistance in two areas.

The first, he explained, was from a personal standpoint. He and his wife had adopted their little girl from China a few years earlier. Because of this, he understood what was involved in the process and was available to offer any advice or guidance. He continued by saying he was also aware that we had run into a financial stumbling block and thought that perhaps he could help us from a professional angle.

He had spoken with his editor and they wanted to do a "warm fuzzy Christmas story" about our adoption. He hoped it would raise awareness of Chinese adoption and would, perhaps, generate some financial support from the community. We scheduled an appointment to do an interview on December 22nd.

Then just a few days later on December 14th, I received an e-mail from a reporter at one of the local television stations. He said that he had found out about our efforts to adopt our daughter and would like to meet with our family to do a story. I responded to his e-mail and said that we would be happy to meet with him. We scheduled an appointment for the afternoon of Monday, December 18th.

Just after I finished responding to the reporter, I noticed it was time to leave for our Christmas luncheon that was planned for the investigations division of the police department. Our Sergeant was treating us all to lunch at the Great Wall China Buffet.

After we had each made three or four trips through the buffet line, we all settled back, stuffed to the gills. The waitress brought us a plate of fortune cookies and we each took a cookie from the plate. The detectives took turns sharing their fortunes.

My turn came and I opened my fortune and read, "YOU ARE ABOUT TO EMBARK ON A MOST DELIGHTFUL JOURNEY." I smiled from ear to ear, pleased but not surprised, that my fortune had a great message inside it. After all, the Turners had a track record of receiving wonderful fortunes.

The anxiety and apprehension that had been consuming my body for the last few weeks were completely calmed by this sweet message. I had been somewhat nervous about the trip, having had a fear of flying for many years. All the fear had been suddenly replaced by a great peace of mind.

Fu Dan, a girl who can bring you luck. This little girl had been part of our lives for only two weeks, yet she was already bringing us more blessings than we could imagine.

I arrived home from work that evening and had barely set foot inside the door when the telephone rang. It was a television reporter named Deb Nelson. She too had heard about our adoption and wanted to do a news story. She was very anxious to air the story and scheduled an appointment with us for Sunday morning, December 17th at 9:00 a.m.

We were all brushed, polished, and shined when Deb arrived at our home. She was very intrigued by our story, our history, and this little girl that had come into our lives. She interviewed us together and also separately, paying very careful attention to Eric and his feelings about the adoption. She commented that he was very poised for being only 10 years old. Deb was quite amused with Eric and was obviously captivated by the excitement we all radiated. Her interview lasted almost two hours. She thanked us for sharing our story with her and told us to watch the news the following night to see our story.

Round two of our media interviews commenced the next afternoon. Ryan Haslum came to interview us at our home. He was also very interested in our story and interviewed us at length. He left our house shortly before 5:30 p.m., just in time for us to hurry to the television to turn on the news to see Deb's coverage of our adoption story. We recorded the story to keep for our family history and especially to show Marlee when she got older.

Ryan's story followed the next evening on the news. Both stories were done very well and we were very thankful for the time and effort they put into telling the public about our adoption story. We hoped that it would raise awareness of Chinese adoption and perhaps motivate others to do the same. We also hoped that it might generate some donations.

The morning of December 22nd brought John Trumbo from the Tri-City Herald to our home. We had a wonderful visit with him for over two hours. We were able to share experiences with each other about the whole process and he was able to answer our questions about what was ahead of us. He asked about my travel date and we told him we didn't know yet, but we were expecting to hear soon. He smiled and casually said, "What would you do if you got the call this afternoon?" We agreed that it would be the most wonderful Christmas present we could imagine.

That afternoon was very cold and the freezing rain bounced off the pavement. Tim begged me not to make the 11 mile drive to work in the dangerous weather, but I had commitments there I had to keep.

When I arrived in my office I had several messages waiting for me on my voice mail. The first one was from JoAnne Bailey. Her voice was animated as she said, "Shannon, give me a call. I have exciting news for you." It took me over an hour to get through to her because her telephone was busy. My adrenalin raced as each minute passed by, wondering what the exciting news was about.

Finally, at 3:00 p.m., the telephone rang. Jo Anne's excited voice said, "I hear you're going to China! You got your travel approval and your consulate date is set." Hearing the words brought tears to my eyes and a drum beat to my heart as I realized that this wonderful adventure was actually becoming a reality.

Jo Anne explained to me that I would be leaving for China on February 2nd and that my interview with the consulate would be on February 12, 2001. As I heard her say the date of February 12th, it brought back such intense emotional memories I could hardly contain myself. I asked Jo Anne, "Did you say February 12?"

She verified the date, and then asked, "Why, does that date have some significance?"

I explained to her that it was on February 12, 1999, that I summoned all the strength in my body, went to the hospital, and had a hysterectomy. I couldn't believe that the most discouraging, heart-breaking date of my life was now going to be one of the happiest dates of my life.

I thought back to two years previously, as I was lying in a hospital bed. At that time I was wondering why the Lord had put me through the pain and heartache of years of infertility. I had no idea that two years from that day I would be sitting in front of the U.S. Consulate in China adopting my beautiful daughter.

The red threads continued to reach out from our little Marlee waiting for us half way around the world. The week after Christmas I received a telephone call from Marlee Middleton, the lady I had met at the kitchen show earlier in the month. I had sent her a copy of the journal I had been keeping about our adoption experience.

She explained that her holiday season had been very busy and that she hadn't had a chance to read the journal until recently. She and a friend had been reading it together when they came upon the account of the day of our referral, November 28th. Marlee said she gasped as she recognized that very important date.

"Shannon, you'll never believe this. November 28th was the date my adoptive parents brought me home from the hospital!" The tears flowed down my face. November 28th was the day she came into their lives; and it was the day our Marlee came into ours.

The miracles didn't stop there. One evening as I was cleaning up after doing yet another kitchen show, I was visiting casually with a few of the ladies who had attended the party. Tim and I had been associated with these ladies for many years and they were familiar with our family's history. They were asking questions about the progress of our adoption and were enthusiastic about every aspect of it. One lady asked when I would be traveling and I gave her the dates. Then I added the disclaimer, "But I won't be going anywhere if I don't come up with the rest of the money."

I briefly explained our situation and the ladies agreed that it was quite a mountain to climb. One of the women interjected and said, "Shannon, if that's all that's standing in your way, you can borrow the money from me!"

There was silence in the room and I stared at her in awe, wondering if I had actually heard what she just said. I was beyond words as my mouth hung open. She continued, "I'd be happy to loan it to you. Just let me know how much, and we'll work up an agreement for you to make monthly payments to me."

The tears welled up in my eyes and I fought to find the right words to express my gratitude. "You have no idea how you just changed my life," I whispered through the tears. I threw my arms around her and told her how much I appreciated her generosity. She told me that she was happy to help and that the money was available for us whenever we needed it.

I drove home that night with renewed hope, feeling a peace that I had been in search of for months. This angel was the answer to our prayers. We would continue to raise as much money as we could on our own, but after we had exhausted all our resources, I knew we could go to her for the rest.

Our Christmas was incredibly sweet as we made memories with our extended family and shared our excitement for my upcoming trip to China. We envisioned the next Christmas when we would have our little girl in our family and shared ideas about how she would enjoy it.

The article about our adoption appeared in the local newspaper just before the New Year. It was very well written, very touching, and included a beautiful photo of our family. The only thing it didn't include, however, was any mention of the need for financial assistance. We were a little disappointed that the reporter had failed to include that information. At the very least, we had hoped it would give the name and location of Marlee's Orphanage Fund. Just like everything else we had encountered throughout the process, things didn't exactly

go as we had planned.

ON YOUR MARK, GET SET, GO!

It was now 2001; time to start making travel plans and packing for my incredible trip across the world to bring our daughter home. I was feeling on top of the world and had energy to spare.

My first visit to the audiologist showed nothing wrong with my ears. In another attempt to try to solve my dizziness, my doctor put me on steroids. They didn't seem to help my dizziness, but they certainly gave me the energy I needed to get everything accomplished that I needed to do.

Chris and her husband, Brian, were visiting from Seattle the weekend of the 5th of January. She was six months pregnant with their miracle baby boy through the amazing procedure of in vitro fertilization. We had been infertile together for years, and now we were both awaiting our babies.

Our family had a wonderful weekend visiting with Chris and Brian. On Saturday night we had a late dinner, made snacks, and settled back to watch a movie. I had just turned off the lights and started down the stairs into our family room when all of a sudden my feet went out from under me, and I landed on my tailbone on our oak stairs.

The pain raced through my body like lightning. I thought I was going to throw up, and then I quickly changed my mind and thought that fainting was a better option. Trying to maintain my dignity in the presence of company, I opted not to spew obscenities and just held my breath.

Everyone rushed to my side, although my blurred vision didn't allow me to distinguish who was who. My tailbone started to throb and Chris rushed to get ice for me. Tim helped me to a lying position on the floor. The only thing I could think of was that in just twenty-six days I was going to be flying to China, and now I was going to be making that flight on a very sore rear end. My world had gone from euphoric to desperate in a matter of seconds. I spent the rest of the weekend with my tail end on ice, wondering what else could possibly be thrown in my path.

Monday morning came, along with the rest of my life. I had commitments galore that week, and there was no way I could spend it laying in bed. So I dragged my literal sore butt out of bed and spent the morning doing a search warrant at work. I tried not to bend, sit, lift, or cough. It's difficult to effectively carry out a search warrant with those restrictions.

The following two days I taught a law enforcement class at a local technical school. The high school students laughed at the way I walked and sat very gingerly, and especially at the fact that I had to carry around my "donut" to sit on. I told them that was what they had to look forward to when they got old; your body falls apart.

The following day I went to the audiologist for round two of my ear tests. The hour-and-a-half test concluded with a very painful, nauseating test. It consisted of a probe stuck into my ear with a small balloon at the end, which the doctor slowly inflated. The first time it was filled with cold water, then again with warm water. The more it inflated, the dizzier I got. It was awful. The doctor informed me that he would submit his findings to my physician within a week.

Friday was the end of a very discouraging, painful week. My whole body hurt and I just wanted it to go away. I had so much to do to get ready for my trip, but every move my body made was excruciating. Eric had been home sick from school all week, so I was also trying to take care of a very sick, grumpy little boy in addition to pampering my tender backside.

As the day progressed, my chest started to feel very heavy and I began coughing. I coughed and coughed and coughed. I coughed all night. I coughed so hard in the morning I threw up. I was sick, and I didn't want to face the fact. I kept asking myself "Why?" and couldn't come up with an answer.

My dear friend, Lenise, had been planning an adoption shower for me for several months and it was scheduled for that morning, January 13th. I put on my happy face once again and went to the shower. After all, the guest of honor couldn't be sick.

I had 42 friends and family members shower our little girl with gifts that morning. It was the beautiful highlight of my otherwise gloomy week. Marlee received so many wonderful gifts: clothes, shoes, socks, coats, hats, dolls, toys, books, stuffed animals, sheets, blankets, and on and on. For three hours I forgot how miserable I felt and just basked in the love of my family and friends.

I came home from the shower and went straight to bed. I coughed and slept for the next two days. I finally pulled myself out of bed on Tuesday morning and crawled into work. I looked and sounded really awful. I tried to exercise the "mind over matter" trick and just continued to do what had to be done. The dizziness was still a big obstacle. The audiologist's report didn't reflect anything out of the ordinary, so my doctor decided to have an MRI done to see if it would shed some light on the problem.

During that week I received all my travel plans from Great Wall. Friday I received my plane tickets from the travel agent, then the rest of my itinerary was faxed from the adoption agency. I swallowed a big reality pill as I looked at my plane tickets, hotel reservations, and detailed itinerary. The adventure I was about to embark on was in black and white, and I was holding it in my hand. In just 15 days I would be on an airplane heading for China, and I would finally meet the daughter I had dreamed of for so many years.

HEART STRINGS

My goal was to be packed and ready to go by Sunday, January 28th. I didn't want my last few days at home to be rushed with last minute packing that would add stress to my already stressed out life. I had been meticulously packing for two weeks. My packing list was four pages long and very detailed. Each night I would go down the list and put a few more things in my suitcase.

I was feeling much better by then. The MRI had shown that I had a sinus infection and my doctor put me on antibiotics. In just a few days, I was beginning to see a light at the end of the tunnel. I wished they'd gone that route back in October and saved me the hassle of all the painful, expensive tests. A $5.00 bottle of antibiotics was finally what solved my problem.

Finally, on Saturday, January 27th, after sitting on my suitcase to get it zipped, I was finished and ready to go! And I was even one day early! The next five days were going to be relaxing as I enjoyed them spending time with family and friends and leisurely saying my good-byes. I should have remembered that things never go as planned.

On Sunday morning our family attended church just as we did every Sunday. That day was a little out of the ordinary, however, because my parents were going to be the speakers in the church service. I knew my mother had been fretting and worrying about it for weeks, and I prayed silently to myself that she would be able to get through it, meeting the very high standard that she placed on herself.

My mother is a perfectionist, and I have been accused many times of inheriting that quality. I still haven't decided if it is a blessing or a curse. For years, I knew that Mom put the unnecessary burden upon herself of memorizing speeches. This time was no different, and I knew that she had spent hours rehearsing her talk.

As the service continued and it was time for her talk, she walked to the podium, looking beautiful and composed as she always did. She started very eloquently, and I smiled as I listened to her talk. It reminded me of the years she spent teaching me about public speaking and the essential elements of a good speech.

She continued with her talk for several minutes, and then became a little emotional. At first I didn't think anything of it, because it's very common to shed a tear when talking about spiritual things. But I soon had a very disturbing feeling come over me as I watched her and listened to her words. They didn't flow the way they usually did, and she seemed a bit confused. To anyone else listening to her talk, they would think she was just emotional about the subject matter. But I knew my mother's personality like the back of my hand, and I knew that there was something wrong.

At one point in her talk, she paused for a few moments in silence. She struggled to find the words she had rehearsed and appeared a little disoriented. She repeated her last few lines, but still couldn't get on with her talk. She hesitated again, then apologized and reached for her notes. I knew that she must be very nervous or emotional to resort to her notes, because that was the cardinal sin in her book.

She read the remainder of her talk, then ended it and sat down in her seat. I watched her rest her head on her hands and knew that she was very frustrated with herself.

My father proceeded with his talk and the meeting ended. After the meeting, I was distracted by many friends who wanted to wish me well on my trip, so I wasn't able to attend to my mom as quickly as I had hoped. At one point I saw her sitting in a chair in the foyer looking very tired, her head resting on her hands. I thought that was unusual because she would always rush from one meeting to the next, never taking time to sit down.

I was approached by yet another friend wishing me luck on my trip, when I felt a tug at my dress. It was Eric, who had been sent to deliver a message from Tim.

"Dad says to meet him outside right now. He needs you."
I rushed outside to see my husband and father, who stood
either side of my mom. They each had her arm and were
helping her to the car.

A long time family friend who was a nurse, came
rushing to me from the direction of my family. She
looked me directly in the eye and said, "Shannon, you
need to take your mom to the hospital. I think she has
suffered a stroke." The words shocked me and I couldn't
believe what I had just heard.

I hurried to my mother's side to assess the situation
and come up with a plan. My father would drive her to
the hospital, and I would meet them there after I had
dropped off Tim and Eric at home.

I had always been thankful for my wonderful family,
but that afternoon made me realize even more what

incredible siblings I had. My two brothers and their wives came to the hospital immediately. My sister waited by the phone to do whatever was needed. We spent the next six hours waiting, worrying, talking to the doctors, and most importantly, praying.

Mom seemed to be in stable condition physically, but she had no recollection of what had happened, where she was, or why she was there. The doctor confirmed that she had, in fact, suffered a mild stroke, known as a "TIA." It had affected her short-term memory. He couldn't tell us how long it would last or if the damage would be permanent.

After many hours, the doctors determined she was stable enough to be released. They sent her home with medication and guidelines to rest and follow up with her family doctor the following day. I returned home that night wondering how I could ever get on a plane in four days and travel halfway around the world, leaving my dear mother behind, not able to help take care of her.

The following day I spent making phone calls to my mother's doctors, collecting paper work, and accompanying my mom and dad to the doctor. I went to and from work in between those appointments. I realized that my presence at the doctor really wouldn't solve anything, but I felt I needed to be making some type of contribution during those four days before I left. Once I got on the airplane, I would no longer be able to help my family.

I came home from my parents' house that evening tired and worried. I was so overwhelmed with emotion I wanted to collapse. At about 10:00 p.m. the telephone rang. It was Tim's twin brother, Tom. He had called to tell us the status of their father.

Tim's father, Russell, had been diagnosed with leukemia back in October. At the time, the doctors predicted he would not live until Christmas. He had been responding well to blood transfusions, however, and was still holding his own in the latter part of January. We had been praying that he would live long enough to meet his new granddaughter.

But Tom had called to tell us that their father had taken a drastic turn for the worse, and they were not expecting him to live much longer. The people from the hospice were attending to him, but we should expect him to go soon. Although we knew this day would come, it was still very difficult to hear the words.

Not only was I going to leave my mother who had suffered a stroke, I was now also going to leave my husband to bury his father. During the previous months I had imagined what would happen when his father passed away. I envisioned myself helping with food, making arrangements, and playing my cello at his funeral.

Now I wasn't going to be able to help Tim's family with anything, and most importantly, I wouldn't be there to offer support and comfort for Tim and Eric. I had been waiting for almost a year for this trip to China, and now the strings of my heart were pulling in so many directions, I was numb.

I spent the following days praying and pondering. I shared my concerns with Tim about feeling like I was abandoning my two families in their most desperate time of need. During one of our conversations he said to me,

"Shannon, there are a lot of people here who will take care of your mother. And whether you stay or go, my father is still going to die. There are many people here who can make the arrangements for his funeral. But there is only one person who can be Marlee's mommy, and that's you. We all have our jobs to do, and yours is to go to China and bring our daughter home."

Shannon G. Turner

THE DAY THE LORD HATH MADE

The morning of February 2, 2002 started at 3:45. That's "o-dark hundred" in cop talk. I had gone to bed just before midnight and had awakened three times during my three hours and 45 minutes of "sleep." Needless to say, I didn't feel very rested as I crawled out of bed and dragged my exhausted, anxiety-ridden body into the shower.

My night had been filled with strange dreams about my trip to China. Every time I would nod back off to sleep, another bizarre dream would awaken me. The last one, I remembered, was actually very funny, and I related it to Tim as I washed my hair in the shower.

I had just arrived at the hotel in China. My guide escorted me to the beautiful, spacious lobby and told me my daughter would be arriving any moment. My body shook with anticipation. Suddenly, the doors of the hotel opened, and I saw several Chinese nannies walking in holding children in their arms. I searched through the crowd to find my daughter.

My guide touched me on the shoulder, pointed to a large pillar, and said, "Look, there is your daughter." From behind the pillar peeked a beautiful little girl holding a nanny's hand. Her head was bowed and I could only see the top of her hat. Then her little face looked up, and I gazed at a beautiful, blue-eyed, fair-skinned little girl with long, curly blonde locks.

I did a double-take, squinted to focus, then asked my guide, "Are you sure she's Chinese?"

My guide nodded her head emphatically like a bobble-head doll and replied, "Oh yes. She Chinese girl."

I studied the little girl once again, shrugged my shoulders, and responded, "Okay, if you say so." I then rushed to my daughter and gathered her into my arms.

Tim and I laughed together at my dream and continued scurrying around preparing for my trip. The anxiety that raced throughout my body was consuming. This was the day I had held in my heart and mind with great anticipation, not just for the last 10 months, but for 10 years. I had expected to be giddy with excitement and happiness, but the gamut of emotions I had experienced in the preceding days had left me exhausted and numb.

I was emotionally torn, concerned about my mother and also broken hearted that I was leaving my husband to bury his father while I was in China. Yet, this was supposed to be the most exciting adventure of my life, so I should have been on cloud nine. But I didn't know what to feel. Even if I could have somehow decided on which emotion to settle on, I didn't think I had the strength to even feel it.

I hurried to get myself ready. I had one hour to go through my checklist for the umpteenth time, pick up my niece, Elis, who was accompanying me on the trip, and get to the airport on time. Tim and Eric helped me do one last search to make sure I hadn't forgotten anything. Once again I carefully counted the $7,000 in cash I had taken out of the bank the day before, divided it and labeled it for each expense, then tucked it inside my money belt and strapped it to my stomach.

As I secured the money to my body, I again said a prayer of thanks for our dear friend who had loaned us this precious money. We had earned and saved as much as we could, but ended up taking her up on her offer to borrow the remainder that we needed for the trip and expenses. She was the answer to our prayers.

As I closed the front door of the house, I realized that I was leaving my home for two weeks and was about to travel half way across the world. I was bringing home our daughter, and our lives would never be the same.

We arrived at the Pasco airport at 5:12 a.m., exactly one hour before the flight was scheduled to leave. We checked in at the registration desk and checked our luggage all the way through to China. Seeing the tag that read "Beijing" on the suitcases was somewhat surreal. It still hadn't really hit me that when I ended this trip in approximately twenty hours, I would be in China.

At 5:30 a.m. we had a wonderful surprise as my parents walked through the doors of the airport. They had come to see us off and wish us luck. My brother,

Kent, who was Elis' father, had also come to wish us well. At 5:50 the call was made to begin boarding our flight. The anxiety raced through me like a lightning bolt. I felt like I was going to be sick.

Elis was already saying her good-byes. I turned to my parents, gave them hugs and kisses, and then finished with Tim and Eric. I was overwhelmed with emotion, so I turned and quickly exited through the doors and walked out onto the tarmac.

Our airplane sat waiting for us, outlined against the black sky. As I made my way up the steps to the plane, my body was filled with the wonder and excitement about the journey ahead of me. I didn't know what the next two weeks had in store, but I prayed that the Lord would be my strength and help me accomplish this overwhelming task.

Elis and I looked at each other and said, "Here we go!"
I was so thankful that she was joining me on the trip. It
would have been ideal if Tim and Eric could have
accompanied me, but it was all we could do to financially
afford my trip. Tripling that amount for all of us to go
would have been impossible. Elis was twenty-two, single,
and adventurous. There was nothing physically or
financially keeping her from going, so she quickly
accepted my invitation to share in my adventure to
China.

The flight from Pasco to Portland reinforced my
hatred of flying. We were barely in the air when the
turbulence started, and it rocked the little sixteen-
passenger plane back and forth with ease. The feeling I
had was reminiscent of our summer vacation to
Disneyland and our ride on the roller coasters. Also being

quite prone to motion sickness and feeling nauseated already, I shuddered at the thought of enduring turbulence all the way to China. I closed my eyes, said a prayer, and asked the Lord to please give me the strength to endure the trip ahead of me.

Most rides at Disneyland last only just a few minutes, but this turbulent roller coaster lasted for sixty-five long minutes. I was relieved when we touched down in Portland and I could walk on ground that wasn't moving. Unfortunately, our next flight left in just twenty-five minutes, so Elis and I quickly found our way to the next gate and arrived just in time to start boarding the plane.

The next airplane was much more comfortable than the previous one. It was a 737 and a person could actually stand straight up in the cabin without hitting their head on the ceiling. We settled into our seats and prepared for our flight to San Francisco, which was scheduled to be just under two hours. We had barely reached cruising altitude before I was sound asleep.

The sound of the "fasten seat belt" tones woke me up as we descended into San Francisco. It was a beautiful, sunny day and the Bay area was beautiful. I was hoping that the remainder of our flights on the trip would be as smooth and restful as that one had been. Famous last words.

It was 9:30 a.m., and our flight to Beijing was scheduled to leave in just over two hours. We grabbed a bite to eat before our next flight, since we had decided it might be the last identifiable meal we would eat for quite some time.

After we finished lunch, we found our way to our departure gate and checked in with the attendant at the desk. We sat at the gate trying to get some rest, but at the same time work out any wiggles we had before getting on a very cramped airplane for twelve hours. The thought of the long flight was overwhelming.

Fortunately, I was blessed once again and didn't seem to be having any distressing problems with my ears or my sore behind. I was incredibly grateful for that. At 11:15 a.m. they made the boarding call, so we gathered our things and boarded the Boeing 777 destined for China.

BEIJING

We had been in the air for twelve hours and my watch said it was just after midnight. The pilot announced that the current time was 4:00 p.m. on February 3rd in Beijing. My body was telling me it was way past my bedtime, but our new clock said I had another six hours before I could go to sleep. My body was winning the battle.

Stepping off the airplane and into the Beijing airport was culture shock at its best. I felt like a very tiny fish that had jumped from its secure little bowl into a great big sea. To make matters more uncomfortable, I happened to be a goldfish in the middle of a large school of eels. I stood out, to say the least. People stared at us everywhere we went.

We made our way through the ocean of people that filled the beautiful new airport, passed through many security checkpoints to show our passports, and then finally arrived at the baggage claim. After finding our bags, which were surprisingly intact and all accounted for, we saw an adorable little Chinese woman standing at the end of the room with a large green flag that read "GWCA." She introduced herself as Maggie, a guide from Great Wall China Adoption. She was there to take us to our hotel in Beijing. The thought of a bed that I could lay down on was heaven!

We met up with the other families that had come in on our flight, loaded up our luggage, and made our way to the bus. The cold Beijing air hit our faces and took our breath away. It had just started to snow, and the falling flakes were picturesque against the Beijing skyline. I tried to take it all in as we drove into the city, but my eyes kept closing from exhaustion. Before I could completely fall asleep, our bus came to a stop and Maggie explained that we would have to walk from there. A short hike led us to the lobby of our hotel. It was spacious, elegant, and an oasis at the end of a long trip.

We quickly checked in, found our room, and flopped our tired bodies onto the beds, which were only slightly softer than concrete. I didn't care at that point. I was horizontal and not moving, and that's all that mattered. Many of the families were going to meet for dinner, but we were too tired to eat.

Elis and I found our way to the business center of the hotel, sent a short e-mail home to let everyone know we had arrived safely, then went to bed at 7:00 p.m. China time. I was too tired to figure out exactly what time it was back home. I just knew it was late and I was tired. My exhausted body melted into my hard bed and I was sound asleep in a matter of seconds.

At 4:00 a.m. my rested body woke me and I tossed and turned in my tiny little bed. This was my welcome to time zone adjustment. I tried to go back to sleep, but just became more frustrated. I sat and listened to the sounds of China outside out hotel room and wondered what our first day in China had in store for us.

At breakfast that morning we met the other Great Wall families who had flown in the night before. It was nice to finally put faces with names. The breakfast buffet was quite intriguing, but I was able to find some pastries and fruit that looked fairly palatable. After we finished our breakfast, we boarded our tour bus and set out for a day of sightseeing.

Our first stop was Tianamen Square and the Forbidden City. It was still snowing from the night before and we estimated the temperature to be around 5 degrees after attempting to convert Celsius into Fahrenheit. Tianamen Square was enormous. Snow covered the ground and Chinese music played over the loud speakers in the square. Our guide, Matthew, gave us historical information as we snapped photos and soaked up the incredible ambiance of the place where we stood.

We couldn't stand still for long, however, as our toes started to get numb. We quickly walked toward the entrance of the Forbidden City. Had it been summer time, we would have walked around the entire square and enjoyed more of the sights, but it was almost painful to stand still for more than a couple of minutes.

We entered the Forbidden City and were overwhelmed by its vastness. Matthew explained to us that the Emperor would sleep in a different room each night, and he was twenty-seven years old before he slept in the same room twice. I could easily understand how a person could live there and never have to set foot outside its walls. I tried to take myself back in time and imagine what life was like inside the walls of the city. It stretched as far as the eye could see in every direction.

Midway through the Forbidden City, we increased the pace of our tour from 33 to 45 rpm's. We were all freezing cold. After a couple of hours all the rooms started looking alike and we just wanted to be warm! Finally, just before noon, our guide announced to us that our tour was over and we would board the bus for lunch, then on to the Great Wall of China. We all cheered at the thought of heat and food!

We enjoyed a warm thirty-minute drive to a local restaurant. Our first authentic Chinese meal was quite delicious as well as entertaining. Ten of us sat around a large round table. In the center of the table was a large revolving disc where the servers placed our food. When they finally finished delivering our food, the table was full of beautiful, mouth-watering dishes.

Nothing had given me the heebie-jeebies so far, so I felt like the meal was a success. But then, just as I thought I had successfully completed my first authentic Chinese cuisine, a waitress brought out a plate, set it on the table, and announced to the crowd, "Fish." Yes, it was. It was the whole fish.

Before I left the United States, I made a vow that during the trip I would not eat anything that looked back at me. He was definitely staring his dead, beady little eyes in my direction. I passed on the fish, but others in our group decided to dig in.

The fish platter was on the outside of the revolving disc, and every time someone would spin the center of the table to get the platter, the fish's tail would hit my water glass. After being flogged by this fish tail several times, I finally dramatized a little tizzy fit. Terry Biggs, who was sitting beside me, proudly announced he would take care of it. He reached over, tore the tail off the fish, and took a big, crunchy bite out of it. The entire table cringed in unison as they exclaimed, "Eeeewwwww!"

After our meal, we had an hour to shop at the Friendship Store that was adjacent to the restaurant. Elis and I were so excited to shop, we set out on a dead run! We buzzed around like bees going from vases to jade, tea sets to jewelry, and dolls to clothes. I picked up a few gifts for friends, but mostly just enjoyed studying the beautiful quality of Chinese merchandise. I was especially intrigued by the beautiful jade and purchased a chess set for Eric. He had loved chess for years and I knew this would be a beautiful set that he would love his entire life.

The group met back at the bus warm, fed, and gratified by a little retail therapy. We were all excited for the second half of our day, the Great Wall of China! With the exception of meeting my daughter, the Great Wall was the one thing I was the most excited about seeing during my trip.

The bus continued on its way out of Beijing towards the mountains. It was still snowing, and we had been warned that the condition of the highway to the Great Wall was somewhat unpredictable because of the weather. We traveled about an hour, then came to a complete halt. Many cars and buses were stopped in a line on the road.

Our guide and driver left the bus and walked toward the front of the pack of vehicles. They returned quite some time later and announced that the road had been closed due to snow and ice and we would be unable to go to the Great Wall.

There was a simultaneous, disappointing, "Ohhhhhhh!" throughout the bus. We were all very discouraged and some even suggested we walk, however the distance to the wall was over three kilometers and it was very mountainous. With the weather, the temperature, and the lateness of the day, there was no way we could go.

My heart sank as I realized I wouldn't be able to see the Great Wall. We were so close, but still too far away. I resolved quickly that there was nothing I could do about it and reminded myself that Marlee was the purpose of the trip to China, and everything else was just frosting on the cake.

I was a little consoled, however, when our guide said we would be stopping at a pearl factory on the way back to Beijing. Buying a strand of pearls was the third thing I was most looking forward to. So to console my grief over not being able to go to the Great Wall, I bought three strands of pearls, two pairs of earrings, and a bracelet. Who says happiness can't be bought?

We arrived back at our hotel at 6:00 p.m., cold and tired. Some of the other families in the group wanted to get together for dinner, so Elis and I joined them. It was too cold to walk anywhere, so we decided to try out the restaurant there at the hotel.

We discovered the challenges of ordering from a Chinese menu, then trying to get assistance from waitresses who didn't speak any English. Our dinner was very good, for the most part, with a few interesting things that were more entertaining than palatable. We laughed at our own ignorance of Chinese customs and food. At one point we realized we were the only people in the restaurant making any type of noise at all. We were sure the people there in the restaurant were either very entertained by us or extremely annoyed, but we weren't quite sure which.

At any given time we had at least three employees of the restaurant standing around our table waiting to assist us. I dropped my napkin on the floor and before I could bend over to pick it up, one of the ladies swooped in, picked it up, and replaced a new napkin on my lap. I occasionally saw a little glint of a smile on one of their faces as they watched us try to identify what we were eating.

Knowing that the following day was going to be long and emotional, we ended our evening early. Elis and I stopped by the business center to check our e-mail and send a quick note home. The e-mail I was anticipating was waiting for me.

Tim's message told me that his father had passed away Friday night, the same day I had left for China. Just as I had feared, Tim was left to handle the burden of burying his father by himself. I remembered the words Tim said to me before I left about how we all had our jobs to do. I was thousands of miles away from home and unable to physically do anything to help. I knew all would be well at home as they grieved over the loss of my father-in-law. I had a very important job to do in the morning, so I crawled into bed and slept with anticipation of meeting my daughter.

"GOTCHA" DAY

The telephone rang at 5:00 a.m. I searched for it in the dark, picked it up and put the receiver to my ear upside down. A very pleasant voice spoke to me in Chinese. The only thing I understood was, "hello, good morning." I looked at the clock and suddenly the reality of the day woke me up like a cold shower. This is the day I would fly to Shenyang and meet my daughter.

We had to leave the hotel by 6:15 a.m. in order to catch the bus to the airport. Elis and I hurried to get dressed, then ran downstairs to the restaurant to get some breakfast. I have always found it difficult to eat when it is so early that it's still dark outside. I forced down a piece of toast and some juice, then went back up to retrieve our luggage. After checking out and loading the bus in the snow, we were on our way back to the Beijing airport.

Once we arrived at the airport, the 17 Great Wall families all went their separate ways. They were being divided up to travel to four different provinces to get their children. Six families went to Jiangsu Province, eight went to Hunan Province, one family to Guangdong, and two families to Liaoning. All the provinces were in central or southern China, with the exception of Liaoning, where we were going. The latest weather reports of Liaoning recorded temperatures of 35 degrees below zero. I had been warned two weeks prior to leaving, so I had come armed with my warmest clothing.

We all said our good-byes and gave each other our best wishes until we saw each other again down in Guangzhou. Elis and I, along with Clyde and Brenda

Scott and their daughter, Maggie, headed off to our departure gate. A guide from Great Wall China Adoption, Jeanne, would meet us in Shenyang and see us through our week there.

Our flight left on schedule at 7:50 a.m., and it was a very short one-hour flight to the city of Shenyang. When the pilot announced we were descending into the Shenyang airport, I looked out the window at the world into which my daughter had been born. The sky was gray and the ground was white. It looked cold, miserable, and very poor. It appeared very much the same as Siberia had when we had flown over it.

The plane touched down and we soon came to a stop. As I walked down the steps of the airplane, the piercing sub-zero weather smacked me in the face. Taking a deep breath made my lungs hurt, and I couldn't bear to look up into the wind.

All the passengers were herded into a large bus that took us to the airport terminal. The buildings of the airport looked old and war-torn. The walls and floors were cold, gray concrete, and there was no heat in the building.

An airport employee approached us to retrieve our luggage claim tickets. Fortunately, Clyde Scott took care of the luggage for us. I was so cold I couldn't move. I buried my hands in my pockets, pulled my hat down tight over my ears, and bowed my head. We followed a sea of people through long halls to a lobby. There we met our guide from Great Wall China Adoption, Jeanne, and her 14-year-old daughter, Tiny, who was on winter break from school.

We guided our luggage carts out of the airport and across a parking lot that was covered in ice several inches thick. The driver encouraged us to get in the van while he loaded our luggage. I didn't argue with him. I felt like my brain was freezing from the bitter cold. I found a seat in the van and crouched into a ball to try to glean some of my own body heat. The others did the same and the only thing that could be heard was our teeth chattering.

The first twenty minutes on the van were silent as it took our little group into the city of Shenyang, the capital of Liaoning Province. We were trying to thaw out and regain our senses after being exposed to the bitter elements.

Jeanne explained to us that Shenyang was an industrial city with a population of six million, the fifth largest in China. A dirty film covered the snow and ice as far as I could see. As I looked at the city surrounding me, all I could think about was the fact that I couldn't wait to get my daughter out of this place. The thought of spending a week in this bitter cold was quite discouraging.

The driver delivered us safely to our warm oasis, a brand new, very modern hotel. The employees were sweet and gracious and welcomed us with open arms. It was straight up 10:00 a.m., and our daughters were to arrive in just thirty minutes.

Elis and I hurried to our room to drop off our luggage and gather Marlee's things. My heart was pounding and I thought I was going to hyperventilate. Elis kept me sane and organized, helping me find all the things I had brought to entertain Marlee. Just before 10:30 the telephone rang. I picked it up and heard Jeanne say, "They're here!"

I let out a scream and started shaking. I jumped up and down excitedly repeating the words, "They're here! They're here!" I raced out the door and down the hall to Jeanne's room. Elis followed behind me with all the important things that I had forgotten: the camera, my backpack, the video camera, and gifts. I couldn't think of anything except that I was about to meet my daughter.

The door was slightly ajar and I heard many people inside the room. I knocked on the door and pushed it open at the same time. The room was filled with many adults, who I assumed were from the orphanage, plus Jeanne and Tiny.

Standing directly in front of me were two little girls dressed alike in layer after layer of warm clothing. Jeanne said to me, "Do you know which one is your daughter?" I looked at the two little girls standing side by side and almost took a step back.

The girls were dressed identically from head to toe. They wore black insulated pants and orange jackets with leopard print trim and matching hats. I blinked and stared at the two little girls. Attached to the bottom of their hats were long, blonde curls! It was just like my dream! My daughter looked like she had blonde curls.

I immediately recognized Fu Dan from the photos I had spent the last two months memorizing. She was much taller than I had imagined. My body started to shake and my eyes filled with tears. I opened my mouth, but nothing came out. One of the ladies from the orphanage took my daughter by the shoulders, moved her towards me, and said, "This is your mother," in Chinese.

I crouched down in front of her and said, "Hello Fu Dan. I am your mommy," the way our guide, David, had taught me to say it the night before. I saw a look of fear in her eyes and she began to cry, which prompted the other little girl to cry also. The women from the orphanage all rushed to their aid and attempted to comfort them. Instead, the girls just cried harder, which started a chain reaction.

The orphanage ladies cried. I cried. Elis cried. We all cried. I tried to comfort my daughter by wiping her tears, but she just pulled away from me and hugged the leg of the women standing beside her. I took her hand and walked to the bed, then lifted her onto my lap. I hugged her tight and again said to her, "Wa sher nee MaMa. Boo Koo."

I really hoped I was saying, "I am your mommy. Don't cry." For all I knew, I was saying, "My clothes are dirty, will you wash them?" I repeated myself over and over through my own tears. She continued to cry and kick, and I didn't know what else to do but repeat the only Chinese phrase I knew and try to comfort my daughter.

A woman from the orphanage tried repeatedly to calm Marlee down, and her words seemed to give her some comfort. I glanced over to the other side of the room and saw Clyde and Brenda Scott doing the same thing with their daughter, Fu Xi, who would be named Chloe Rose. She was equally as hysterical as Marlee.

After just a few minutes, Jeanne announced to us that it was time to go to the civil affairs office to start the paper work for the adoption. We gathered the wailing girls and our belongings, then made our way to the lobby of the hotel where the bus was waiting for us outside. Marlee had stopped crying now and allowed me to hold her hand, but she would not acknowledge me or look at me.

We braved the sub-zero wind for a few moments and loaded the girls onto the bus. Marlee sat on my lap, her tear-stained face pointed toward the window in a trance, with an occasional sob forcing its way out of her little body.

After just a few blocks, we stopped in front of a tiny photo shop. Jeanne explained to us that we had to first get photos taken of the girls for their passports and notary certifications. We piled out of the bus and into the photo shop that consisted of two very small rooms. There were 14 adults and two screaming children. It was so cramped you had to step outside if you needed to change your mind.

It was Marlee's turn first. An employee led Marlee and me into the back room and showed us where to sit on a stool. The first photo was of both of us together. I held her on my lap, pressed my cheek to hers, and tried to force a smile on my own tear-stained face. All the other adults were standing behind the camera trying to make Marlee smile. Their attempts were in vain, however, because my little girl wasn't going to smile even if her life depended on it. The second photo was of Marlee by herself, and I ridiculously joined in with the crowd to try to get her to smile. She gave a very solemn, brave pose for the camera.

We exited the room to make way for the Scott family and Chloe. I took Marlee back out into the front of the store and searched my emotional brain to find something to break the ice with my daughter. I remembered the backpack that I had filled with goodies and unzipped it while Marlee watched.

The first thing I found was a bag of fruit snacks, which I opened and offered to Marlee. By this time, Chloe was done with her photo session and had joined us. Marlee took the fruit snacks from me and immediately offered them to Chloe, who took one and popped it in her mouth. I tried to get Marlee to eat one, but she continued to feed them to Chloe until the package was empty.

I then pulled out a red and white striped cloth bag that held twelve finger puppets my sister, Camille, had made. I put them on my fingers and both girls were immediately intrigued. They both held their fingers out for me to put the puppets on them. They started to play and talk to each other, and for the first time since we'd met, they seemed to be completely distracted from the emotional upheaval they were in.

We waited quite a while for the photos to be printed, but the wait was softened by the entertainment of the finger puppets. After we finally obtained the photos, we loaded into the bus again for our next destination.

Once again, Marlee sat quietly on my lap, her eyelids heavy and her head nodding. Before long, she was sound asleep in my arms. Her nap only lasted a few minutes, however, because we had arrived at the Civil Affairs office.

I picked her tired little body up in my arms and strained to make my way down the stairs of the bus. The curb was covered in black, thick, bumpy ice, and it took all the strength I had to keep my balance and carry her weight at the same time. We filed into the building and made our way up several flights of stairs to the Civil Affairs Office. We all crowded into a small room that was furnished with a desk, a computer table, two couches and a coffee table.

Jeanne started explaining all the paperwork to Clyde and me. He and I sat crouched around a small coffee table, filling out form after form that was printed in Chinese. The people from the orphanage assisted the civil affairs employee with their end of the paperwork, while Brenda, Maggie, Tiny, and Elis played with the girls and entertained them.

Marlee tried hard to ignore me, but I would occasionally see her look at me out of the corner of her eye. When I would smile at her or make any type of overture, however, she would scowl and hug the leg of one of the nannies. I did my best to ignore her from her perspective, but watch her out of the corner of my eye at the same time. She stood by the desk and watched all the papers being signed, stamped, and handed around. I could tell she was a very perceptive little girl by the way she watched the proceedings.

The noon hour rolled around and we were all hungry, so we pooled our resources and came up with a lunch that consisted of fruit snacks, goldfish crackers, breakfast bars, and water.

After our meager lunch, one of the nannies from the orphanage started the girls singing. They stood side by side and sang song after song, bowing graciously after each one. It was obvious that the girls had been very well taught and cared for as I watched them sing and interact with the nannies from the orphanage. I had forgotten to bring my video camera and was kicking myself for it, but

Clyde had his and video taped it for all of us.

When the paper work was finally finished, the civil

affairs officer presented me with the Certificate of

Adoption that was placed inside a beautiful red folder.

She handed it to me and said, "From now on, she is

yours." She also gave me a letter from the Dandong

Welfare Institute that thanked us for adopting Fu Dan and wished us good health and happiness. Along with the letter, we were given a beautiful jade pendant of an ox, representing the year Marlee was born.

Elis took pictures as I collected all the documents and gifts. I thanked all the officials in my teary, emotional voice and assured them I would love my daughter throughout her life.

I then presented the orphanage director with the $3,000 required donation. One of the nannies counted it and asked me to place it in the bank envelope for her. They made out a receipt for me and thanked me again.

Jeanne informed us it was time to distribute the gifts we had brought. We handed them out very formally: the director first, followed by the nannies, then the civil affairs director. They were all very gracious and thanked us for our kindness. Lastly, I handed a bag of gifts for the orphanage children to the director. I explained to her that my co-workers at the police department had donated these items to the children in her welfare home and I hoped she would find a use for them. She took the bag graciously without opening it.

It was well after 2:00 p.m. by then, and we were all tired and still hungry. I had hoped we were done with the paperwork, but Jeanne explained to us that we had to now go to the notary office. The thought of more papers made me shudder.

Again we all piled onto the bus and headed to another office building. Marlee sat on my lap once more. After traveling just a few blocks, her eyes closed and she started to snore. My poor little daughter was exhausted from her traumatic day. I closed my eyes as well and rested my cheek on her head.

After just a short 10-minute ride, the bus came to a stop. I carefully scooped Marlee into my arms, trying not to wake her. When the cold air smacked our skin, however, her eyes opened and she struggled in my arms. I set her down to walk, took her hand, and guided her into the building.

When we entered the ground floor of the office building, I would have sworn it was a vacant building that had been condemned five decades ago. It was dirty, run down, without heat, and the paint was peeling off the walls. We walked up three flights of stairs to the notary office. There we sat for the next two hours until our papers were completed.

The girls were becoming a little more personable, and Marlee would let me entertain her by singing and feeding her dried pineapple. The orphanage director sat across the room and watched our interaction with each other. Marlee and Chloe were remarkably good for having sat in offices for the last five hours, gone without lunch and their naps, and been thrown into the arms of perfect strangers.

Finally, at 4:30 p.m., they announced to us that we were finished with paperwork for the day. We carried our tired girls out to the bus again for our trip back to the hotel. Again, Marlee let me hold her on my lap as she stared out the window quietly.

The bus had traveled only a few blocks when it came to a sudden stop. Without warning, all the people from the orphanage got up in unison and stepped off the bus.

Both Marlee and Chloe instantly realized what was going on and went into hysterics.

I tried to console Marlee, but she was so out of control I could barely hold on to her. She kicked and screamed and tried to wiggle out of my arms. I was trying to keep her from falling onto the floor of the bus, and it took every ounce of strength I had to keep her on my lap. She was a very strong little girl, and she hit me and kicked me with all her might. She was crying and screaming, sobbing the same thing over and over in Chinese.

I turned to Jeanne and asked her what she was saying. Jeanne listened to Marlee's words between her sobs and translated for me. "Take me back. I want to go back!" Jeanne tried to talk to her and console her, but Marlee kept telling her that she didn't want to go to America, she wanted to go back to the orphanage. She explained to

Jeanne that she was scared and frustrated because she didn't understand anything I was saying and she feared I would abandon her.

My heart was breaking for this scared little girl. I asked Jeanne to explain to her that we had been waiting for her for a very long time and that her daddy and big brother were very excited to meet her. She had a house, a room, and a family who loved her. Jeanne interpreted this information to Marlee, but it didn't seem to make any impact on her.

Still sitting on my lap, she turned around and looked at me, the tears streaming down her face. Her eyebrows were pinched together and her eyes were piercing. She stared into my eyes and began to scream at me in Chinese. I didn't understand a word she was saying, but I completely understood the tone. I looked to Jeanne for translation. She hesitated before telling me, then said, "She says, 'Take me back to the orphanage and find another little girl.'" I felt my heart break and couldn't contain my emotions any longer. I buried my head behind her back and quietly sobbed.

We finally arrived back at our hotel. The Scott family took Chloe to their room to get to know each other. I felt there were a lot of things Marlee and I still needed to talk about to put her mind at ease, so I asked Jeanne if she would mind interpreting for me once more.

We went to Jeanne's hotel room where it was quiet with no distractions. Marlee sat on the bed and I knelt on the floor in front of her. I had Jeanne explain to her all the things that were waiting for her in America. I told her again how long we had been waiting for her to be part of our family and that we loved her very much.

Jeanne spent quite some time explaining Marlee's new life to her. She seemed to listen and comprehend what she was being told. She turned to Jeanne and asked, "Will she promise to bring me back to visit when I'm grown up?" I had no choice but to assure her that I would bring her back to her birth land. It seemed very important to her. I looked my daughter in the eye and promised that I would bring her back to China when she was older.

Marlee sat quietly for a moment and seemed to be processing all the information she had just heard. The look on her face told me that she was softening and was somewhat satisfied with what she had heard. Marlee then looked at Jeanne and asked her a question. Jeanne smiled and turned to me to translate. "She says, 'But when I come back, everyone will be so old.'"

Jeanne's eyes widened as she looked at me. "You've got a smart one on your hands!" she exclaimed.

After Marlee and I felt like we'd said all there was to say for the time being, Jeanne told Marlee that it was time to go with me to our room. She didn't resist at all and walked out of the room with me. I took her hand and we walked down the corridor of the hotel.

As we stepped inside our hotel room, she looked around inquisitively. It was apparent from the look on her face that she had never seen a room so beautiful before.

As we began to get settled in our room, I noticed my poor little girl was sweating from head to toe. I took off her coat, which I hadn't been permitted to do previously. The nannies had been very strict about making sure she was bundled from head to toe. Under her coat was another coat. I helped her off with her shoes and the heavy black snow pants she was wearing. Taking her pants off revealed a pair of heavy quilted pants, under which was a pair of green knit leggings, which covered a pair of long johns. Then three sweaters later, I found a little girl underneath, substantially skinnier than she had appeared to be with all those layers of clothes on. I wrapped her in a towel and carried her to the bathroom.

I started a bubble bath and sat on the edge of the tub with her on my lap. She was still apprehensive about making eye contact or talking to me. When the tub was full, I carefully placed her amidst the bubbles. She was a little scared at first, but after a few minutes she started to relax.

I sat on the floor of the bathroom and played with her throughout her bath. Without her realizing it, she started to acknowledge my existence and interact with me. After an hour, I was soaked and she was shriveled like a prune. She seemed exhausted and hungry, so I lifted her out of the tub, dried her off, and ordered dinner from room service.

Getting my new daughter dressed proved to be an unexpected challenge. She was much taller than I had expected, therefore most of the clothes I had brought for her were too small. Her pajamas were in that category. I had brought the kind that had feet and zipped up the front, but her legs were so long, she couldn't stretch them out in the legs of the pajamas. She wrinkled up her nose and looked at me bewildered. I took them off and searched for something that could act as pajamas for the night.

Fortunately, I had brought a pair of long underwear for her. They were none too big, but they would do for the time being. I then proceeded to evaluate the rest of the clothes I had brought and discovered that she could wear only one pair of pants and three of the shirts. All the shoes and even the slippers were too little. I was grateful that the next morning was set aside for shopping because I had to completely start over for her. I made a pile of clothes to give to her friend, Chloe, who was much smaller than Marlee.

Our dinner arrived from room service just as we finished our fashion show. I had ordered a club sandwich that included ham, turkey, bacon, and chicken, hoping there would be something she would like. We were comfortable with each other sitting there in the middle of the bed, so I didn't want to interrupt the good thing we had going.

I put the plate of food on the bed between us, and she immediately eyed the pile of french fries that accompanied the sandwich. She picked up a fry and offered it to me. She then offered one to Elis. Finally, she ate one herself. That quickly became the routine and again I was reminded that my daughter was first concerned with the welfare of others, then herself.

After she devoured the entire plate of food, including the lettuce and tomato that was added for garnish, we played with the finger puppets again. She put them on her fingers and insisted I kiss each one of them, then start all over with the first one again. Soon we started a tossing game with the puppets, and before we knew it she was hurling everything she could find at both Elis and me. She would laugh hysterically when we couldn't catch something. It was comforting to see her finally smile and laugh. It had been an exhausting, emotional day.

Finally around 9:00 p.m., Marlee started to yawn. I took her into the bathroom and brushed her teeth, helped her to the bathroom, then told her in my very best Chinese that I had just learned that afternoon, "It's time to go to sleep." I wrapped her up in the pink blanket I had brought for her and cuddled her for a few minutes, then laid her in her crib that was next to my bed.

I changed into my pajamas, crawled under the covers of my own bed and we stared at each other for a few moments with our heads on our own pillows. She pulled her little arm out from underneath her blanket and stretched it towards me through the bars of her crib. When our hands met, she squeezed my hand, smiled, and closed her eyes. Within a few minutes she was sound asleep.

GETTING TO KNOW YOU

Marlee woke up from a restful night's sleep, stood up in her crib, and reached her hands up for me. We spent a few minutes cuddling and wiping the sleepies out of her eyes. I still couldn't believe I was actually holding *my daughter* in my arms. It was surreal. She continued to be quiet and reserved, but allowed me to help her get dressed, brush her teeth, and see to her needs without crying or resisting.

We had breakfast in the hotel restaurant on the second floor. It was the most elaborate breakfast buffet I had ever seen. There were literally dozens of dishes to choose from: bacon, ham, eggs, sausage, potatoes, pastries, breads, vegetables, seafood, cereal, yogurt, juices and on and on. Marlee ate and ate until I thought she was going to pop. I finally had to push the food away from her and tell her that it was time to go. We had a date with the Scott family to go shopping at 10:00 a.m.

Jeanne took us to a very nice shopping mall that was near our hotel. It was six stories high and very elaborate. From the bottom floor we could see up the middle to all the levels above.

With Jeanne's direction, we found our way to the top floor where the children's apparel was located. Marlee took off like a stereotypical woman on a shopping spree. She ran from one thing to the next, holding up outfits and smiling with satisfaction. I didn't look at anything for very long before she was off to something else. We went through each department several times before I could get her to sit still long enough to actually try something on.

The most beautiful outfit caught my eye above everything else. It had black pants with red pockets and a beautiful black and red crushed velvet jacket with a black fur collar. I knew Marlee would be stunning in it. The price was 188 yuan, which converted to about $23. An outfit like that in the States would have been well over $60.

After deciding which size would be most appropriate, I took it from the rack. As if out of nowhere, three store employees surrounded me. They all spoke rapidly in Chinese, pointing and carrying on. Finally, one took me by the hand, led me to a counter, and helped me understand that I had to pay for the item before I could take it from the department. I paid my money to the cashier and returned to the clerks with my receipt. They took a copy of my receipt, then placed my purchase in a bag and handed it to me. I had just been initiated into the world of Chinese retail.

As we roamed the department store, we discovered a wonderful play area for children. For only 25 yuan, about $3.00, the children could go in and play to their hearts' content.

I took my shoes off and accompanied Marlee into the play area. She took off like a bullet and escaped into her world of childhood imagination. The Scotts soon discovered the play area also, and Chloe joined Marlee in bouncing, sliding, riding, and jumping. For two hours they both escaped from the trauma that had been introduced into their lives the day before. They were just happy playing together as best friends who didn't have any cares in the world.

Clyde Scott volunteered to play with both girls while Elis, Brenda, and I went shopping again. It was much easier to make purchases without the assistance of my very busy daughter.

We finished our shopping and went back to the play land to rescue Clyde. The girls were getting hungry, so we gathered their things and made our way down the very crowded escalators to the first floor for an authentic Chinese lunch...McDonald's.

It was a sight unlike anything I had ever seen before. The restaurant was a typical McDonald's, but there were at least 300 people crammed into it, pushing each other to get to the front to order. I had noticed previously that the Chinese didn't form organized lines like we tend to do in the United States. It was pretty much a free-for-all.

We decided that it would be best if Clyde and I stood in line and ordered for everyone else, while the others took the girls and waited in a place that wasn't quite so crowded, which was an oxymoron in China. I had yet to find a place that wasn't crowded.

After what seemed like eternity, we finally arrived at the counter to place our order. Of course, the entire menu was in Chinese. Fortunately they had a picture menu, so Clyde and I just pointed to the item we wanted and held up fingers to indicate how many we wanted. Just as I was about to order, Tiny, Jeanne's daughter, came up behind me and said, "Excuse me, Mrs. Turner. Your daughter wants ice cream."

In all the advice I had received before leaving for China, I had been cautioned not to give the children cold food such as ice cream or ice in their drinks. They were not used to it and it would be a shock to their system. I had to laugh to myself, however, because I was quickly learning that my daughter certainly did not fit the profile of an average three-year-old girl from an orphanage in China.

I told Tiny that I would, in fact, get her some ice cream. She turned to leave, then spun back around again. "Oh, and she says she wants the kind with the chocolate on top." I burst out laughing. My daughter was definitely a girl who knew what she wanted.

We finally got our lunch and found our way back to the bus. We had barely gotten comfortable in our seats before Marlee had inhaled the french fries. It was apparent they were a hit. She spent a little more time on her burger, but only because she was so exhausted from playing all morning. She kept falling asleep between chews.

Fortunately, we arrived back at our hotel within a few minutes. I scooped up my wilting daughter and carried her right to our room. After pulling her coat and shoes off, I laid her down in her crib. She drifted off to sleep the minute her head hit the pillow.

Elis wanted to catch up on her journal, so she offered to stay with Marlee while she napped. That gave me time to go to the hotel business center and e-mail home to everyone. I hadn't had a chance to send any messages home since I had met my new daughter. I was sure that Tim and Eric, as well as all my friends, were dying to find out how our meeting went.

I had many e-mail messages waiting for me from friends and family wishing me well. It was so nice to read everyone's words of love and support, but it made me very homesick. I had only been in China for three days, yet it seemed like forever.

I started my e-mail home and typed a few paragraphs about the previous two days when a nice young gentleman who worked for the hotel approached me. "Mrs. Turner, you have a phone call." He showed me to the phone at his desk. It was Jeanne calling to say that we had to leave to go pick up all the documents from the notary office, so I logged off the computer and hurried to my room to gather my things.

Since the girls were sleeping, Clyde and I made the trip back to the notary office alone with Jeanne. Fortunately, we didn't have to spend as much time in the cold, bare office building as we had the day before.

Jeanne brought us each a packet of documents that was easily three inches thick. They were the official notarized copies of all the documents we needed. The packet included both the Chinese and translated English version of the adoption certificate, notice of adoption, abandonment certificate, and birth certificate. There were four copies of each packet.

We looked over the documents carefully, then paid the officials the $500 notary fee and waited for our receipts. Jeanne congratulated us and said that our paperwork was done until Friday when we would pick up the girls' passports. After that we would be able to leave Shenyang and fly down south to Guangzhou. Just the thought of leaving that frozen city made my heart dance. But it was only Tuesday and we didn't fly out until

Saturday. I was sure my blood was going to freeze solid during those four days.

Jeanne explained to us that she had arranged for us to go sightseeing the next morning with a local guide. The idea of spending hours outside in the sub-zero arctic tundra of Shenyang didn't excite me much, but I tried to stay optimistic. Maybe the city really did have a few redeeming qualities and tomorrow was our chance to see them. Then again, maybe not.

When we arrived back at our hotel, I returned to the business center and finished my e-mail home. I was happy to find Elis and Marlee playing happily upon my return to our hotel room. I was somewhat discouraged, however, that my daughter seemed rather unaffected by the fact that I had been gone. She just casually glanced up at me, then continued on with the game she and Elis were playing. I told myself it had only been one day and I had to give her more time to bond with her new mommy.

It was dinnertime by then and Jeanne had made reservations for us at a nearby restaurant, one that we could walk to via skywalks and didn't have to go outside. We were grateful for that. Maggie, the Scott's nine-year-old daughter, had suffered an asthma attack earlier and was not feeling well, so Brenda decided to stay home with her for the evening. Clyde and Chloe joined me, Marlee, Elis, Jeanne and Tiny for dinner.

We entered the restaurant and were greeted by many beautiful, ornately dressed women. They guided us through the very elegant restaurant to our own private room. I felt like royalty the way they tended to our every need. We let Jeanne do the ordering for us since she could both read and speak Chinese. We figured that was the safest way to not end up eating dog, snake or cockroaches for dinner.

Within just a few minutes they started bringing food to our table. It kept coming and coming until the table was full. The food was beautiful and delicious and we ate until we couldn't eat another bite. Marlee and Chloe were shoveling it in so fast I didn't think they could even taste it. They were perfect little ladies with their napkins on their laps, being careful not to spill a drop.

When our meal was concluded and the bill was delivered to us, I was amazed at the cost. The total for five adults and two children was just over 200 yuan, about $25. We looked at each other in amazement as we had expected $100 or more judging from the food, the service, and the beautiful surroundings. Clyde and I asked repeatedly if that was correct and Jeanne assured us that it was. We agreed that we could happily eat there every night. The food was incredible and the price was right.

After we returned to our hotel room, I entertained Marlee by putting her in the bathtub with the set of colorful plastic dishes that I had bought her that morning. She immediately started pouring water from one cup to the other and babbling in Chinese. She was absolutely precious. I grabbed the video camera and started filming.

Marlee filled each cup and set it carefully on the ledge of the bathtub. As she did, I counted them for her in English. After just a couple times, she started to repeat after me, "One, two, three..." all the way up to 10. I had just captured my daughter's first words in English.

BEAUTIFUL DOWNTOWN SHENYANG

Murphy's law again prevailed, and our scheduled day of sightseeing was the coldest day in Shenyang so far that week. It was well below zero, but we didn't know just how far. At that point, it really didn't matter. The air was cold enough to burn our noses and throats and make our heads hurt if we took too deep of a breath.

We all bundled up as much as we could and piled into the bus as we had so many times before. We told Jeanne that we would be perfectly content to just look at the sights from the comfort of our unheated bus rather than expose ourselves to the frigid elements time after time. She laughed, thinking we were kidding.

Our local guide was a beautiful young lady named Ivy. She was a primary school teacher who was on winter holiday working as a tour guide. She had beautiful eyes, an adorable smile, and was incredibly charming. She seemed to instantly bond with Marlee and Chloe. Her English was rough, but her presentation was poised and most entertaining.

Our first stop was just a few blocks from our hotel at a plaza that displayed an enormous statue of Chairman Mao. The bus stopped in a parking lot and we had to make our way across a traffic circle in order to reach the plaza. The traffic was bumper to bumper and five lanes across. The drivers maneuvered their cars with reckless abandon, not yielding even the slightest to pedestrians that might stand in their way.

We scooped up the little girls in our arms and carefully started to dodge the oncoming traffic. Ivy led the way and shielded herself between the cars and our little tour group. I felt like I was playing the video game "Frogger," and I was playing the role of the frog.

We breathed a sigh of relief when we finally reached the other side of the traffic circle. By that time we were so cold and stressed we were shivering. We carefully walked along the ice-covered ground and posed ourselves in front of the huge statue. After a few photos, we all concurred that we were uncomfortably numb and wanted to return to the bus.

Once again we repeated the dance to get across the traffic to return to our bus. We were all relieved to have made it across without being hit and vowed we would not attempt any more street crossing during the remainder of our stay. We raced for the bus and shelter from the cold. Marlee and I huddled together in our seat to stay warm.

We drove for what seemed like miles, with every block looking the same as the one before. Even if there had been a variance, it would have been hard to tell because the inside of the bus windows had glazed over with ice. Nobody seemed to be looking at the sights, just staring at the floor in an icy trance trying to not freeze to death.

We finally emerged into a rather new looking part of town with large modern buildings and open plazas. The bus drove though a beautifully landscaped park that was blanketed with snow. It carefully wound its way back and forth on the little roads that led through the park. The sun was shining by now and the snow glistened like diamonds.

The bus came to a stop at the focal point of the park, a captivating village of snow sculptures. The beauty of the sculptures sparked our interest and we were actually excited to get out of our shelter to see these beautiful creations close up.

We quickly realized that we had to walk carefully, as the snow on the ground was frozen solid with a sheet of ice. We linked arms with each other and slowly crept from one sculpture to the next. Ivy told us about the sculptures and the Lantern Festival that was currently being celebrated in Shenyang.

Suddenly Ivy's eyes lit up and she asked with excitement, "Do you want to play a game?" Her face contorted as she struggled to find the English translation to explain. "It is a dog, uh, pulling a, uh, chair. You sit on the chair, um, and the dog, uh, pulls you. Do you want to play?"

I'm sure that the rest of the group was creating the same odd visual that I was. I figured that I was only going to be in China once, so I may as well throw caution to the wind and be adventurous. I piped up and said, "Sure, we'll try it." I couldn't wait to see dogs pulling chairs. Everyone else looked at me with wonderment, imagining what I was getting them into.

Ivy led us down to a large field to show us the "game." We quickly discovered the game was actually a sleigh ride pulled by a big, beautiful horse. We all smiled and laughed, "Oh, a sleigh ride!"

Ivy giggled when she discovered her misinterpretation. She smiled and shook her head at her mistranslation. "Oh yes, a horse. It is not a dog."

If we hadn't been cold already, the ride around the track in a horse-drawn sleigh put the proverbial "icing" on the cake. About half way around the track, I came to the realization that it was a very stupid idea to have put these already frozen little girls on a sleigh. I buried Marlee's head into my chest and wrapped my coat around her, then bowed my head to shield my face from the cold air. The horse rounded the track and the driver asked if we wanted to take another trip around. Clyde and I simultaneously and emphatically chorused, "No, thank you!"

We were all miserable by this point and we told Ivy that we would like to make our way back to the bus. She could tell that Marlee and Chloe were pretty close to frozen, so she took hold of the little girls' hands and led the way. As they were walking, Chloe said to Marlee, "I can't feel my feet."

Marlee responded, "I think my toes are frozen." As Ivy translated their conversation, we scooped up the girls in our arms and put our frozen bodies into high gear to get them back on the bus.

We sat on their feet and rubbed their hands to warm up their poor little freezing bodies. I secretly wished our tour of this frozen city was over, but Ivy informed us we were on our way to another destination.

Our next stop was a street named after a prominent political family in Chinese history. Because it was the final day of the Lantern Festival, the sidewalks were lined with beautiful, decorative lanterns. There were huge gates at either end, with many shops up and down the street. We stopped briefly to get out and take photos, but didn't want to expose the girls to the cold air any more.

But in the ever-convenient timing of a toddler, Chloe had to go to the bathroom. Of course when Marlee heard that, she informed us that she had to go also. Ivy volunteered to take the little girls to the bathroom while we took pictures. Clyde insisted that he go with them and I was grateful for that as I watched their heads quickly disappear into the crowd.

The little bathroom group had only been gone just a few minutes when the bus driver started to slowly move down the street. We all looked at each other, wondering what he was doing. The driver drove a few yards, stopped for a few moments, then continued on again. He repeated this ritual over and over, and before long he had traveled over three blocks.

The place we had left Clyde, Ivy and the girls was no longer visible. We were all very concerned they wouldn't be able to find us. More than thirty minutes went by and they were nowhere in sight. I finally suggested that we drive down to find them, when we suddenly saw their heads bobbing through the crowd. Ivy looked frozen and Clyde was carrying both girls. It was apparent that he was upset and I didn't blame him. I was too.

The frozen group finally piled into the bus. Clyde immediately asked us why we had driven away. We all shook our heads and told him we didn't understand it either. We had tried, but couldn't seem to make the driver understand to stay in the same place. Clyde tried hard to subdue his frustration, but I could tell he was extremely angry.

The last stop on our tour of Shenyang was Garment Square, a huge plaza that was easily the size of three football fields. In the center of the plaza was a tall golden

sculpture of three sunbirds. It was modern and beautiful
and glistened in the sun.

Marlee wanted to see the huge colorful balloons that
floated above the plaza and I wanted to get a few pictures.
The rest of our frozen tour group opted to stay in the bus.
I promised them we wouldn't be long as we braved the
bitter cold one more time.

Elis and I took Marlee's hand and we jogged to the
center of Garment Square. We seized a few quick photo
moments, then ran around the plaza singing and dancing.
Marlee had an abundance of energy and ran from tether
to tether trying to pull the giant balloons down.

Before long our fingers and toes started to burn, so we
said good-bye to Garment Square and hurried back to the
bus. Ivy asked if we wanted to continue our tour of
Shenyang. A quick vote determined that we had reached

our maximum touring capacity. The thought of our warm

hotel, a hot bath, and some warm food, was irresistible.

MARLEE THE COMEDIENNE

Another perk about our beautiful, modern hotel was that it had wonderful American food. Ordering from room service was so fast and convenient, and very affordable by American standards.

When we arrived back at our hotel after our tour, we immediately ordered lunch and filled our bodies with warm, delicious food. Marlee was completely captivated by the silverware, showing preference to her fork. She even wanted to eat her french fries with her fork. She discovered that she could eat her food much faster with a fork than with chopsticks, and that silverware was also very entertaining. Eating soon became a game and she delighted in the fact that she was making us laugh.

Her next discovery was the almighty ketchup bottle. She wanted to dip everything she could find in ketchup and feed it to me. Unfortunately, I really don't like ketchup, so I declined and told her it was for her. She then popped the food into her mouth with a very gratifying sound as her other hand was reaching for the next thing to be baptized in ketchup.

Her french fries soon became walrus tusks and she posed while we took pictures of her. When she realized she was the center of attention, she started to dip all her food in her pop: french fries, lettuce, and even her coleslaw, then dramatically drip them into her mouth.

Elis and I watched her eat with a vengeance for over an hour, amazed at how this little girl could put away so much food! I was delighted to see her sense of humor and knew that she would fit right in with our family. I couldn't wait for her daddy and brother to delight in her adorable personality.

Since we'd had such a cold, exhausting morning, we decided to just stay in the hotel and relax for the afternoon. After lunch we were invited down to the Scott's room so the girls could play together. Marlee, Chloe, and Maggie played hard all afternoon while the adults visited with each other. It was nice to be warm, fed, and sheltered from the bitter cold.

At dinnertime, none of us had completely thawed out from our morning of touring to even think about going outside for our meal. Although it was more expensive than the public restaurants, we opted to just stay in the hotel for dinner. We were more than willing to pay for the convenience of not having to brave the bitter cold.

The hotel dinner buffet was just as extravagant as the breakfasts. I stopped counting after fifty different dishes to choose from. Marlee and Chloe ate their dinner as if it was their last, just as they had since we first met them. We decided they were either really good eaters, or they had never had such a selection and abundance of food. I feared it was the latter.

After our meal, Jeanne convinced the little girls to sing some of their songs again. They stood in the middle of the crowded dining room and sang their hearts out. I had my video camera with me this time and was able to capture it all on film. The fact that dozens of people were watching them didn't seem to have an impact on them at all. After each song they would bow politely and the people would clap for them. I could tell that my daughter was going to be a performer.

Later that evening back in our hotel room, I helped Marlee rehearse saying "hello" to daddy and brother, since I had told Tim and Eric we would call that night. Marlee rehearsed everything perfectly, but I had my doubts if she'd actually come through when the real call came. Finally, 9:00 p.m. rolled around and we dialed the dozens of numbers in order to make our call home.

Tim answered the telephone immediately, even though it was 5:00 a.m. there at home. Marlee practically ripped the phone receiver out of my hand. She put it up to her ear and, in the most perfect, clear voice I could wish for, she shouted, "Hi Baba!"

Elis and I looked at each other, stunned and overjoyed. We couldn't believe she actually said it. She kept repeating the same words over and over, "Hi Ba Ba. Hi Ba Ba. Hi Ba Ba." I asked her to count for him and she repeated after me, in English, from the number one all the way to ten. She then said, "Bye Ba Ba," and handed the phone back to me.

I said, "Well, what do you think?" I could tell Tim was crying as he said, "She sounds sweet!" I then proceeded to tell him about all the new things I had discovered about our daughter that day. I could hear Eric in the background and I told Marlee it was her turn to talk to her brother. She repeated the exact same ritual with him as she had with Tim. I was so proud of her.

After we said our good-byes to our family back in the United States, I prepared Marlee for bedtime. We went through the ritual she had already grown accustomed to: brush our teeth, go potty, say our prayers, sing a song, then tuck her into bed. I lifted her over the side of the crib and gently laid her down onto her blankets. I pulled them up over her and said good night to her in Chinese.

It had only been just a few seconds when I heard her shuffling around in her crib. I turned to find my daughter, apparently very particular, at the end of her crib smoothing out the bedding and tucking the sheets into the corners. Elis and I watched in amusement as she made sure every sheet and blanket was perfectly smooth. Then she crawled back up to her pillow, wiggled under the covers, and pulled them up under her chin.

As I started toward the bathroom to change into my pajamas, I heard a very exasperated sigh come from Marlee's crib again. Once again she was back at the end of her crib straightening and tucking. This time she was apparently telling off the sheets in her most emphatic Chinese. Elis and I looked at each other and giggled as we both commented that Marlee was quite an anal-retentive little girl. Everything had to be just so! Elis laughed as she said, "Look, Shannon, she's as obsessive compulsive as you are!"

BONDING

Our fourth day together, Thursday, February 8th, was filled with indications that my daughter was bonding to me. In fact, my e-mail home that day was titled "I think she loves me."

My first sign was at breakfast that morning. Jeanne told Marlee that she was going to be leaving that evening. She asked Marlee if she wanted to go with her to Beijing or stay with her mommy. Marlee gave her answer very quickly, and Jeanne laughed and smiled at her response. "She says she wants to stay here with her Mama," Jeanne explained. My heart melted when I heard her words.

That morning we decided to take the girls back to the department store that had the play area they loved so much. Elis wasn't feeling well and opted to stay in the hotel for the morning and rest, so Clyde, Brenda, Maggie, and I took the little girls out for an adventure.

We decided to be brave and independent by taking our own taxi. Clyde had one of the hotel employees call the cab, then write down the name of the shopping center for us in Chinese on the back of the hotel business card.

I was quite impressed with Clyde's ease in getting around cities. He had been a domestic airline pilot for twelve years and had been to almost every major city in the world. It was comforting to have him in our little group with his vast knowledge of world travel.

Our taxi arrived just minutes after the hotel employee called for it. Clyde got in the front and showed him the back of the business card with the name of the shopping center. Brenda, Maggie, and I piled into the back seat of the cab and put the little girls on our laps. No sooner had the cab driver read the business card when he nodded his head and took off like a bullet.

I closed my eyes and held Marlee tight as the taxi darted in and out of traffic. We had several near misses with other cars, bicycles, and pedestrians. Brenda and I would occasionally look at each other in fear and squeeze our daughters tighter. I said a silent prayer that we would make it through our stay in China without getting into a car wreck. Fortunately, in just a few minutes, the driver dropped us off in front of the shopping center.

We agreed to meet the Scott family at a designated time back at the entrance to the mall. Marlee and I then set off on our own to do some shopping. We received more than a few stares as we strolled through the store, stopping and browsing at all the treasures.

Many people approached Marlee, asking her name and wondering who this fair skinned, redheaded woman was holding her hand. She replied very politely that her name was Fu Dan, and that I was her mama. The people would look at her, then glance up at me, then back to Marlee again with a very inquisitive, puzzled look on their face. Some would just walk away, while others would inquire further.

Because very few of the people spoke any English, it was nearly impossible to explain our circumstances to them. Occasionally a person was so consumed with curiosity, they would go find someone who spoke English to come translate for them. I could see the light bulb go on for them when their interpreter explained that she had been abandoned and I had come to adopt her. Their eyes would widen, a grin would cover their face, and they would shake my hand emphatically. One gentleman told the interpreter that because I was such a generous person for adopting Marlee, I would have health and happiness for the rest of my life.

We bumped into the Scotts as we were shopping, and Clyde again volunteered to play with the girls while Brenda and I shopped. He took Marlee and Chloe into the play area while I finished my shopping.

I was amazed at the things that are so common to us, but are virtually impossible to find in China: crayons, a blow-up ball, warm pajamas, and a tablet of plain white paper to draw on. By now I was an expert at the Chinese retail game and was shopping like a native. Of course, I didn't blend in with the natives. I was the only Caucasian person I saw, other than the Scotts, the entire time I was in Shenyang. I felt very much the minority, and knew that people were staring at me everywhere I went. I soon became accustomed to it, but was always aware that I was the focus of everyone's stares.

I finished my shopping and returned to the play area to spend some time with my daughter. I took my shoes off and joined her in the play area. We went down the slide, jumped in the balls, rode the cars, and had a wonderful time. I didn't realize, however, that a fairly large crowd had assembled outside the wall of the play area, all of them focused on us.

After quite some time of being aware that we were being stared at, a very pleasant Chinese woman approached me and said, "Excuse me. Is that your daughter?" She pointed at Marlee and looked at me, obviously very baffled.

I smiled and replied, "Yes, she is." The woman looked back and forth from Marlee to me, just as all the others had, and said very matter-of-factly, "But she Chinese girl!" I had to fight to keep from laughing, then very politely explained our story once again.

At one point I looked beyond the woman to the crowd that had gathered. Every ear was turned, listening intently to what I had to say. I felt like I was in an E.F. Hutton commercial. When I finally finished my explanation, the woman turned to the crowd and repeated my story to them in Chinese. Almost in unison, the entire crowd sighed, "Ohhhhhh!" and gave me nods of approval. I felt like a celebrity whose fans were waiting to get an autograph as they each approached me and shook my hand.

After the crowd had dissipated, a woman who appeared to be in her mid fifties approached me. She took my hand and put it between hers, looked me directly in the eye, and spewed Chinese faster than I thought a person could speak. She touched my cheek with the back of her hand, then carefully touched my hair and examined my long auburn curls.

Finally, she reached her hand out to the side of her and took the hand of a young man, who I assumed was her son. He looked to be in his early twenties. She joined his hand with mine, smiled from ear to ear, then clasped her hands together and clutched her chest. I wasn't sure, but I had the impression she had just married us.

I smiled at the woman and thanked her, but showed her my hand and pointed to my wedding ring. She just continued to smile at me and clutch her hands to her chest. I waved good-bye to her in an effort to make her go away and she finally waved back to me and walked away with a group of people, looking back over her shoulder the whole way and blowing me kisses.

The girls were getting tired and hungry, so we gathered them up and headed down the six floors of jam-packed escalators to the ground level. I had barely stepped on the escalator when I looked ahead of me and saw the same young man who I had just joined hands with earlier. He grinned from ear to ear and waved my direction. I just smiled and nodded my head politely.

We finally made our way through the sea of bodies to the cold first floor. We braved the frigid air and walked to the street to hail a taxi. To our pleasant surprise, a cab was parked right there at the curb. We opened the doors and climbed in, but the cab driver motioned with his hand, apparently telling us to get out. We were confused by his gestures because we didn't see any apparent reason he couldn't take us. But after several minutes of his continuous refusal, we got out of the cab and stood on the curb again.

Fortunately, there were at least six empty taxis behind him, so Clyde held up his hand to hail another one. The next taxi slowly drove past us and the driver shook his head and waved his hand at us. The taxi that followed did the same, and so on and so on, until at least a half dozen taxis had refused to pick us up.

Brenda looked at Clyde very disgustedly and said, "Honey, I think we're being discriminated against." The little girls were whining because of the cold, so we all went back into the department store. Clyde told us to stay together and wait for him while he went to find someone to help us.

Clyde finally came through the crowd followed by not one, not two, but three uniformed men. I didn't know what type of organization they were with, but it was obviously some type of government law enforcement. Clyde beamed with pride and explained that these gentlemen would gladly help us find a taxi.

We bundled up the girls again and followed the uniformed men outside. They walked with authority to the curb. One of them proceeded into the middle of the street, put his hand out in front of him, and forced a taxi to stop. He leaned in to the driver and explained our circumstances. They pointed at us and talked back and forth for a moment. The uniformed man then opened the door and motioned for us to get in. We piled in as fast as we could, grateful to finally have a ride. I smiled and waved through the back window at the uniformed man who hailed the taxi for us. He smiled back and gave me the "thumbs up" sign.

GREEN LIGHT TO GUANGZHOU

When we returned to our hotel after a busy morning of shopping, Jeanne gave us the news we had been waiting for. Marlee and Chloe's passports were done! This was our green light to finally leave Shenyang.

Clyde and I, along with Jeanne, traveled across town to pick up the girls' passports late that afternoon. We celebrated that night by returning to the beautiful restaurant we had gone to on Tuesday night. Brenda and Maggie had stayed behind in the hotel that night, so we wanted them to be able to experience the wonderful food and atmosphere as well.

As we were walking through the corridors of the hotel on the way to the restaurant, Marlee and Chloe were walking side by side, hand in hand, as they always did.

They were carrying on a very in-depth conversation, apparently about Chloe's new shoes. Jeanne laughed at their banter and gave us a synopsis of their conversation.

MARLEE: "Hey, you have lights in your shoes!"

CHLOE: "Yeah, aren't they cool?"

MARLEE: "My shoes don't have lights in them!"

CHLOE: "That's because mine are better than yours!"

MARLEE: "I want some shoes like that."

CHLOE: "No, you can't have them. They're mine. Besides, your feet are too big!"

We all laughed at how serious the girls were and the way they examined each others' shoes at great length. They continued their shoe conversation all through dinner, after which Marlee announced to me that she also wanted shoes with lights in them.

Jeanne and her daughter, Tiny, caught the train at 8:00 that evening to return to Beijing to meet another group of adoptive parents. We assured Jeanne that we'd be just fine for one more day without her before flying to Guangzhou on Saturday. She had arranged for Ivy to check in with us on Friday to see if we needed any assistance, then escort us to the airport on Saturday morning.

Friday morning was greeted with much excitement, as it was our last full day in Shenyang. We just had to endure one more day of the bitter cold, and then we could fly down South where it was warm. The clock couldn't go fast enough as far as we were concerned.

Marlee and Chloe had a play date planned for the morning to take a bubble bath together. Elis opted to stay at the hotel and relax with the Brenda and the kids. So

Clyde and I, accompanied by Ivy, took one more trip to the department store for some last minute purchases.

It was a sunny, beautiful day. We took a poll amongst the three of us and came to the conclusion that it had probably warmed up to freezing. Clyde and I were fairly amused by the fact that we had no problem at all getting a taxi now with Ivy along. She simply held her hand out and it was as if one appeared out of nowhere. I was sure that it helped that she was Chinese, but I was also sure that it didn't hurt at all that she was drop-dead gorgeous.

As we made our way through the traffic, Ivy explained to us that the taxi drivers all worked for the same company and did not accept tips. We had found that to be common in most of the places we had been so far in China. It was so unusual for us to see people refuse the tips we would offer them. All of our taxi rides, no matter how far we had to travel, had been 7 yuan, which was approximately 90 cents.

When we arrived at the mall, we agreed to split up and meet back at a specific place and time. Ivy and I went over my shopping list and set off to accomplish our goal. It was definitely an asset to have her with me, as she interpreted for me and told the sales people exactly what I was looking for. It cut my shopping time into a fraction of what it had been previously.

Rather than wandering around aimlessly, searching for something in a department store that seemed to have no rhyme or reason as to its organization, Ivy would simply ask an attendant for the location. It sure beat the frustration of resorting to charades in order to explain to the store clerks what I needed. After a week of it, however, I was getting quite good. It was especially fun to shop with Ivy because she and I seemed to have similar interests. We would stop and look at fur coats, jewelry, and all the girlie stuff we could find.

As we walked and shopped, I asked Ivy about the people who worked in the department store. There were so many employees, unlike the stores in the United States. They were all dressed alike in royal blue uniforms. I assumed they received commission, since they would flock to me every time I appeared to be interested in purchasing something. It was as if they were competing with each other to make the sale. But Ivy explained that they all made the same monthly salary, about 400 yuan per month, and they received no commission. I quickly did the math and was stunned when I realized it was only $50 per month. Ivy said that was approximately the same amount that other professions made, including herself. I couldn't believe that she was a primary school teacher with a five-year degree and only made $50 per month.

I asked her how people could afford to shop in a store such as the one we were in. The outfit I had just purchased for Marlee was half a month's salary for the average Chinese citizen. She explained that they only bought what they needed, and never any more. My heart poured out to her and all the other people there when I realized how little money they had to live on. Ivy went on to explain that a good job, which was in management or computers, for example, earned about 2,000 yuan a month. Still, that was only $250.

For the rest of our shopping trip, every time I would purchase something I would think of what that amount of money meant to Ivy and how it was so insignificant to me. It made me realize how much I took for granted the blessings I have and the wonderful country in which I live.

By the end of our morning, I had bought a new camera for myself, toys, a jacket, jeans, socks, and slippers for Marlee, and food for the trip to Guangzhou the next day. I had spent in two hours what it took Ivy six months to earn. I felt guilty for spending so much money in front of her.

When we met up with Clyde again, we decided to be adventurous and walk back to the hotel. Ivy showed us a busy, cobblestone pedestrian street lined with beautiful stores. It ran just two blocks parallel with our hotel. Little did we know that all week we had been so close to such a retail wonderland.

We enjoyed the sunshine on our faces as we took in the ambiance of the bustling stores. I had to stop and take a photo of Kentucky Fried Chicken, all in Chinese, of course, to show my friends back home. Ivy and I stopped many times to take photos of each other on the very picturesque street.

We were quite intrigued with the street vendors selling their wares. As I pointed to some beautiful shoes and made a comment to Ivy, the street vendor mimicked me in sarcasm and repeated my English words in a thick Chinese accent. I just laughed and waved at him.

When we returned to the hotel, we found that Marlee and Chloe had spent the entire morning in the bathtub taking turns dumping water over each other's heads. Elis and Brenda said they had to warm up the water many times for the girls because they had been in the tub so long.

I retrieved my shriveled up daughter out of the bubbles and helped her get dressed. We headed back down the hall to our room to order lunch and start packing.

The three of us enjoyed our evening of packing and playing. Marlee was such a comedian and wanted to play constantly. I would put something in my suitcase, then she would reach in and take it out. She'd then run in the bathroom and close the door, pushing against it so I couldn't get in. We played that game over and over.

Our goal was to be completely packed and in bed by 9:00 p.m. We had to leave for the airport by 6:30 a.m., so our alarm would be set for 5:00 a.m. By early evening, Elis and I were packed, exhausted, and ready for bed.

Marlee, on the other hand, was practicing for her academy award performance. She wanted me to videotape her while she was singing and dancing, then watch herself on video. She'd put her face close up to the camera and make silly faces, then insist we imitate her, sound effects and all. She was quite the creative comedian, and we laughed out loud at her for hours.

Marlee kept up her antics until after 10:00 p.m. Finally, we put her in bed hoping she would get the hint, but she continued to sing and carry on. We must have told her two dozen times to go to sleep, but it had no impact on her. It was hard to be mad at her because she was so funny. Elis and I had to hide our faces in our pillows to keep from laughing out loud, which just encouraged her even more. Finally she fell quiet and we crossed our fingers that she was asleep at last. Just as I started to drift off to sleep, Marlee patted her hand over

her mouth and sang out at the top of her lungs, "Wah

wah wah wah..." The giggling started again.

WE'RE OUTTA HERE!

We were all giddy with excitement at the thought of finally leaving Shenyang. We were looking forward to meeting up with the other families again in Guangzhou and seeing their children. Mostly, we were excited to finally thaw out!

Ivy accompanied us to the airport and took care of getting our tickets, checking us in, paying the airport tax, and checking our luggage. We were sad to say good-bye to her, as she had become a good friend in the few days we had known her.

She had given Marlee and Chloe each a shell from their hometown of Dandong, which Marlee carried very sacredly with her in her backpack. She had also given Elis and me a beautiful post card from Shenyang. She was so kind and giving, we wished we could take her with us for the rest of the trip.

The Shenyang International Airport was packed wall-to-wall with people who were all staring at us as if we had just landed from Mars. Parts of the airport were somewhat modern, but most of it appeared to be straight out of the fifties. Ivy told us a new airport was being built right next to the old one and would be opening very soon. We could see it was very modern and was covered by mirrored glass. It seemed blatantly out of place against the bleak, frozen countryside outside Shenyang.

We found our departure gate very easily and settled the girls into the bright orange plastic seats that sat in a long line. Marlee was quite tired from going to bed late and getting up early. She insisted on going through Chloe's bag that Clyde and Brenda had packed for her, and I was constantly putting things back and trying to distract her with her own toys. An occasional announcement was made over the loud speaker; however, we were now without an interpreter and had no way of knowing what was being said.

I looked at the clock and decided I had time to go to the restroom before boarding. The restroom was only about ten feet from where we were sitting, so I knew I wouldn't have to worry about being gone too long or getting lost.

I entered the restroom, which had no door, and my urgency to relieve myself suddenly disappeared as I looked around me. The floor was cement with a drain in the center. There were two stalls with a step up to each. There were no doors on the stalls, no toilet paper, no sink, and no towels. The "toilet" was a small round hole in the concrete that smelled as if it came directly up from the sewer. My gag reflex was in high gear that day, so I opted not to use the facilities and hold out for the bathroom on the airplane.

As I emerged from the restroom, a sea of people suddenly swarmed to the boarding gate next to where we were sitting. Judging from the time, we assumed they were boarding our flight. As usual, the people were flocked around the entrance in no semblance of a line. We had no desire to throw ourselves into the middle of it, so we just waited patiently until the crowd dissipated.

Despite the fact that a 737 is a large airplane, we felt like we were over-sized sardines packed into an economy-sized can. The people buzzed around trying to put away their luggage and make themselves comfortable. With my twenty-pound backpack on my back, I struggled to make my way down the aisle as I carried Marlee, her backpack, and my carry-on bag. I bumped into people like a ball in a pinball machine, apologizing each time and praying I would soon find my seat.

Finally I plopped Marlee into her seat and stashed our things as quickly as I could. In just a few minutes, the plane was taxiing down the runway. Marlee seemed fairly unaffected by it all until the engines kicked in for take off. She looked up at me in despair with her little face winced, and then began to whimper.

I fastened her seat belt, leaned over, and put my arms around her. I pressed my cheek to hers and started to sing, "Horsey, horsey, on your way; we've been together for many a day..." over and over. I had to sing as loud as I could to compete with the roaring engines.

The plane shot up into the sky like a rocket. Marlee was trying to be brave, but I could tell she was walking that fine line between control and despair. I tried to paint a smile on my face to encourage her, but I was trying not to puke myself. The nausea was overwhelming, so I closed my eyes to see if it would help. I focused on the words of the song and held Marlee as tight as I could.

By the time we reached cruising altitude, Marlee was feeling more secure and allowed me to actually let go of her. I was grateful because my back had a crook in it from leaning over to the side for the last fifteen minutes. I was still very nauseated, so I tried to entertain Marlee with my eyes closed.

After what seemed like forever, the seat belt sign went off and we were finally allowed to get up from our seats. With my bladder aching, I made my way back to the restroom. I was disappointed to see a line at least twenty people long. I knew I couldn't stand in line that long leaving Marlee unattended, so I went back to my seat.

Within just a few minutes, the flight attendants started to make the rounds with breakfast. My pathway to the restroom was now blocked for at least another forty-five minutes. I wished that I had had the nerve to use the hole in the ground back at the airport and prayed that my bladder would hold out.

The breakfast that was served didn't help my nausea much, because the main course had an uncanny resemblance to headcheese. The only thing identifiable or palatable was some fruit, so I snacked on that with Marlee. I amused myself by reading the packaging the food came in, all in Chinese of course, trying to analyze the ingredients. I would give an occasional bite of the unknown substance to Marlee to see how she would respond to it. She would almost always wrinkle up her nose and spit it out, so I felt somewhat vindicated. After all, I hadn't found anything yet that my daughter wouldn't eat.

About an hour into the flight, my nausea went away and the attendants had finished cleaning up from breakfast. The line to the bathroom was again very long and I discovered the reason was that it was the only operating restroom on the entire airplane. I didn't know if my bladder would make it another 2½ hours to Guangzhou. I told Marlee we were going to go potty, even though she said she didn't have to go. She and I waited in line for twenty minutes for our turn. I was surprised that nobody offered to let her go to the front of the line.

After our claustrophobic experience in a restroom that obviously hadn't been cleaned since the Ming Dynasty, we made it back to our seats and I tried to settle back and relax for the rest of the trip. Just as I closed my eyes and exhaled, Marlee felt a sudden urgency to know where Chloe was. She promptly stood up in her seat and shouted at the top of her lungs, "Fu Chiaaaaaaaaaa!"

The plane became alarmingly silent and I felt as if every eye turned to us. So much for trying to be incognito. Chloe stood up in her seat and waved back at Marlee. I gestured to Brenda to have Chloe come back and sit with us so the girls could visit without calling attention to themselves.

Chloe took the window seat, Marlee sat in the middle, and I caged them in by sitting in the aisle seat. I got out the finger puppets and the girls started to play happily. I would tell them the name of each animal in English and they would repeat it after me.

A very sweet young lady leaned forward from the seat behind me. She asked my name and why I was in China. I explained the whole story as I had many times before. I had to keep from laughing when she turned to the people behind her and apparently repeated my story. They all leaned in as they listened to her, then looked at me in unison and nodded with approval. I smiled and said, "Thank you" in Chinese. I was quite amused by their inquiring minds.

The woman continued her conversation with me and admired the finger puppets my sister had made. The girls had turned around in their seats and were giving her a little zoo puppet show. Fortunately, she and the other people were very patient and would giggle at the girls as they played. At one point the woman said, "Your daughter is very noisy."

From her comments that followed, I interpreted that to mean that Marlee was very outgoing. She went on to say that she thought I was very patient with Marlee and that I was a good mother. At one point she initiated a conversation with Marlee and they talked together at length. She then said to me, "She says that she is very happy that you are her mother."

My heart melted. All the frustration, disappointment, hard work and prayer I had endured in the past several years suddenly seemed to disappear when I heard that my daughter was happy that I was her mommy.

BEAUTIFUL GUANGZHOU

The rest of the flight went quickly as the little girls played and I conversed with the woman behind me. Before I knew it, the flight attendants announced that we were descending into Guangzhou. I looked out the window to a beautiful city that reached as far as the eye could see. The noon sun shone over the tall buildings, beautiful green trees, and the sparkling Pearl River winding through the city.

In spite of Marlee's protest, we had to send Chloe back to her own seat with Clyde and Brenda, and then fasten our seat belts. As the plane descended into Guangzhou, Marlee once again gave me that "I don't like this" look. She reached over, grabbed my arms and wrapped them around her, then buried her head in my lap. She started to hum "Horsey, Horsey" again, so I took her cue and sang until we had landed and were stopped at the arrival gate.

We knew our final days in China were going to be pleasant ones when we stepped off the plane and felt the warm breeze blow through our hair. Elis and I looked at each other, gave each other a high five, and simultaneously exclaimed, "Yes!"

We had served our time in the frozen hell of Shenyang. We were now in heaven for the next six days. We quickly shed our coats and sweaters, and with renewed energy we took the girls by the hand and walked through the vast Guangzhou airport. We walked and walked, then walked some more. I didn't think the airport would ever end. Finally we reached a checkpoint where we had to show our passports and fill out entry papers; we then proceeded down the escalators to claim our luggage.

To our surprise, we were greeted by Maggie. We had been told that all the Great Wall guides were busy that afternoon, so we would be met by a bus driver. Maggie was excited to meet Marlee and Chloe and said that she had heard all about them from Jeanne. Jeanne told her they were the smartest girls in the whole province, and the cutest too. Of course, we all had to agree with that.

The bus driver helped us maneuver our luggage out of the airport and across the street to our bus. Elis and I were giddy with excitement as we looked at the beautiful flowers, plants, and palm trees that lined the streets. I kept closing my eyes and turning my head towards the sky to feel the warm breeze on my face. Marlee and Chloe were dancing around the parking lot and exploring the beautiful foliage. They seemed as excited to be in the warm weather as we were.

All the way to our hotel we chattered on and on to Maggie about our stay in Shenyang, reiterating how cold it was and how grateful we were to be there in Guangzhou. We stared through the bus window at the beautiful sights going by. Elis and I would see something and point, then go on to the next discovery. "Look at that!" we'd say to each other over and over.

Marlee wanted to feel the warm air, so I slid down the bus window and let her put her hand out to feel the warm breeze. The most adorable smile filled her face as the wind tousled her hair and she gazed at the beautiful city around her.

The bus came to a stop at the place I had been dreaming of for the last year, the world-renowned White

Swan Hotel. It was at least twenty stories high and sat on the bank of the beautiful Pearl River.

We walked into the lower lobby of the hotel and Maggie helped us check in. Once we had our room keys, we wound our way through the beautiful stores that were located there on the lower level of the White Swan. We rounded a corner and, there in front of us, was one of the most beautiful sights I had ever seen.

An enormous waterfall fell three stories down to a river that ran along the first floor. The skylights above illuminated the beautiful plants and trees that lined the river. A red bridge spanned the river and hundreds of koi swam under it. The sound of the waterfall filled the air.

Marlee instantly ran to the bridge and pointed to the fish excitedly. I knelt beside her and said, "Fish." She looked up at me with a smile and clearly repeated, "Fish." Marlee was so intrigued by it all, I had to drag her away so we could get settled in our room. I promised her we would come back, but she shouted, "Fish! Fish! Fish!" all the way up the elevator.

As we stepped off the elevator onto the 11th floor, a beautiful woman greeted us and showed us to our room. Simply stated, our room was elegant. The view was spectacular, with windows looking north over Guangzhou. The room was clean, bright, and tastefully decorated. The wood was light maple and all the glass was beveled. The closet had fluffy robes and slippers for us. Where the floor wasn't carpeted, it was marble.

Even the bathroom was elegant. The walls were light marble with beautiful mirrors, paintings, lights, and a black marble counter. The brass fixtures gleamed in contrast with the marble. The bathroom even had piped-in music. All we had to do was turn the dial on the wall to choose our style of music.

After thoroughly inspecting our room and oohing and aahing, we discovered the only thing wrong was the fact there were only two beds, and they were as small or smaller than a twin bed. There was no comfortable way for Marlee and I to share a bed.

I opened the door into the hall and the lady who had escorted us to our room immediately came to my service. I explained to her there was no bed for my daughter. She seemed rather confused, so I did my best to make her understand through gestures. She finally nodded and took me into the hall to show me what their children's cribs looked like. They were very small and obviously made for infants. Marlee was way too big for it. I shook my head and thanked her.

I decided to call the front desk and ask for their assistance. After being transferred several times, I finally reached someone who spoke English. She informed me that I could rent an additional bed for $24.00 (American) a night. I declined quickly. I told her that for $150+ per night that I was paying for my room, they should be willing to accommodate my daughter. My complaint was in vain. There was no way I was going to pay an additional $120 for a bed, so I resigned myself to sleeping on the floor for the next five days.

We were tired and hungry, so we decided to check out the room service there at the White Swan. Just as everything else we had found so far there, it was exquisite. The young man who delivered our lunch even seated us and put our napkins on our laps.

My lunch came with a wonderful bowl of clam chowder, which Marlee ate every drop of. She even licked the bowl. That was when I discovered my daughter was a soup addict. It shouldn't have surprised me, since she had inhaled everything else I had put in front of her since we'd met.

Later that afternoon, all the families met in the lobby for instructions from our guides. It was like a homecoming to see everyone again and meet their babies. We all gave hugs and congratulations as we greeted each other. David and Maggie, our guides from Great Wall, divided us into two groups and explained what our itinerary was for the rest of the week. After a few basic instructions, they dismissed us for the evening to get settled.

I asked several of the families if they wanted to get together for dinner. We had all heard about Lucy's, a restaurant just down the street from the White Swan, that served American food. We unanimously agreed to dine there. It was a very comfortable two-block walk, and we were all distracted by the wonderful stores along the way. We agreed we would have to stop and shop on the way back.

Lucy's seemed to me to be something that belonged on a tropical island in the South Pacific. We sat outside at round tables under large umbrellas. The tables lined a sidewalk that ran the length of a beautiful park along the Pearl River. Old Abba songs played over the speakers, and the palm trees swayed in the gentle breeze. We all enjoyed visiting with each other and sharing our individual experiences of meeting our daughters. We ate, visited, and laughed for over two hours.

On our journey back to the hotel, Marlee complained that she was too tired to walk, so I introduced her to piggybacks. That was a big mistake. She thought that was great fun and that began her refusal to walk anywhere for the next five days. It was much easier for me to have her on my back than carry her in front of me, however. And with her on my back as opposed to walking, I always knew where she was.

Elis, Marlee and I enjoyed window-shopping as we strolled back to our hotel. By the time we finally reached the White Swan, it was almost 10:00 p.m. The thought of having to sleep on the hard floor didn't excite me at all, but neither did the idea of sharing a tiny little bed with a three-year-old octopus wearing boxing gloves. Marlee's arms and legs flailed around madly when she slept.

But as luck would have it, Elis discovered two very large, thick comforters in the bottom drawer of the cabinet in our room as we were preparing for bed. We folded each one into three layers and made Marlee a very cozy bed between our beds. She thought it was wonderful, and I was relieved that I didn't have to sleep on the floor. It might have been more comfortable, however, as the beds were just slightly softer than concrete.

TOURING

We strolled into the dining room around 8:00 a.m. to have our first White Swan breakfast. What a breakfast it was! I had never seen such a vast, elegant assortment of food. It put the buffet in Shenyang to shame! The tables of food stretched almost the entire length of the dining room. There was an ambiance I had never experienced as we ate our breakfast sitting by a three-story waterfall. In the other direction, the panel of windows looked out on the beautiful Pearl River. It was incredibly enchanting.

A chef in the dining room made me a beautiful ham and Swiss cheese omelet. My adorable daughter took one look at it and promptly ate every bite. Big surprise! I was beginning to learn that I should take twice the food I intended to eat. My daughter helped herself to my plate as if there was an open invitation posted beside it. I enjoyed watching her eat, but wondered to myself what the food had been like in the orphanage, if she had gone hungry some days, and what her little mind was thinking of all the abundance of food.

We met the other families in the lobby at 9:00 a.m. and set out for our first full day in beautiful Guangzhou. Now that we had our children, our group filled two buses. David's group took one, and Maggie's had the other. The buses drove through the streets of Guangzhou as David told us about the history of Chinese religion.

He explained that most of the older Chinese people were either Buddhist or Tao, while the younger generations mostly had no religious faith at all. He said there were some Christians in the country, although they were the minority. I thought to myself how sad it was that millions of young people had no faith at all. It had been my faith that had brought me to China. It was my faith that gave me the strength to endure the trials I had been given throughout my life. I couldn't imagine what life would be like without it.

Our first stop was at Six Banyan Temple. The pagoda stood several stories high, although we were unable to see it due to renovations being done. The entire structure was surrounded by scaffolding.

The first area we came to was for lighting incense and saying a prayer. David explained that the custom was to light three sticks, representing a prayer for yourself, your family, and the child you were adopting. I thought it would be a cultural memory for Marlee and I to do that together, so I handed the video camera to Elis to capture the moment on film.

We waited our turn to light the incense, then proceeded to the altar to say our prayer. I prayed to the Lord asking for health for myself, happiness for my family, and a life of love for Marlee. We secured our incense sticks in the sand and then joined the rest of the group.

We continued on to the main temple where three large statues of Buddha were the focus. They were easily three stories high and appeared to be completely covered in gold. The room was ornate and incense filled the air. Velvet-covered benches lined the area in front of the statues. David explained that the monks wanted to say a special prayer on behalf of the children to wish them health and happiness in their new lives. They chanted and played instruments for quite some time as our group sat quietly and enjoyed the experience.

Shannon G. Turner

When they finally finished, I was in the same type of trance I had experienced every time I listened to Bolero. I was able to capture some of it on videotape, but opted not to film the entire "ceremony" in consideration for future viewers. I didn't want to be the talk amongst our friends when they warned each other about being invited to the Turners to watch home videos of Chinese monks chanting for three hours.

On the way back to the buses, Marlee and Chloe were enchanted by all the mandarin orange trees. They desperately wanted to pick the oranges, but I feared that was some type of Chinese felony that would put me in prison for 30 years. I deterred their interest and headed them back to the bus. By now the day was bright and warm, and we started to shed our sweaters. Marlee and

Chloe danced around with delight not having to wear so many layers of clothing.

The next stop on our tour was the Chan Family Temple. David took the group through the grounds giving a wonderful history of the temple and the family. I wished that I could hear what he was saying, but I was so busy chasing Marlee and Chloe, I didn't get to enjoy the whole presentation.

The girls had found three ceramic planters that were filled with water and goldfish swimming about. By the time I caught up to them, both girls had pushed up their sleeves and were elbow deep in the water. They were busy laughing, splashing, and saying "fish" over and over.

The girls were having the time of their lives, so I told the Scott family and Elis to go on and take the tour; I would stay and play with the girls. They ran from one fish bowl to the next, then chased each other around the courtyard trying to flick water on each other.

As I watched them out of the corner of my eye, I admired the beauty of the craftsmanship of the temple, the exquisite landscaping, and the magnificent blooms on the trees. Occasionally I would convince the girls to stop running long enough to pose for a picture; then they would take off again to the fish and start the game over again.

The final item on our day's agenda was shopping. The bus took us up very steep, winding streets to a beautiful shop. It had everything imaginable. There was jewelry of every type, dishes, clothes, fabric, teapots, dolls, and on and on. Just like all the other retail shops we'd visited, we were immediately surrounded by sales clerks.

Marlee turned into a literal bull in a china shop, and I couldn't put her down for a moment without her wanting to run and pull something off the shelf. When I pulled her back and told her no, she would scream and throw herself on the floor. I could tell it was going to be a challenging shopping expedition. After an hour of trying to shop and wrestle with Marlee, I finally took her out to the bus and left her with Elis, who had finished her shopping.

I made my purchases and returned to the bus about ten minutes later. As I stepped onto the bus, I heard Marlee sobbing. She saw me, reached out her hands, and cried, "Mama, Mama!" Elis told me that Marlee had become completely distraught when I had left her. It was the first time Marlee had ever shown any emotion over me leaving or returning. I was sad that she was so upset, but I was touched that she had become so attached to me in such a short time.

Marlee clung to me for the rest of the day and wouldn't let me out of her sight. When we returned to the hotel from our sightseeing, we joined several other families and walked back down the street to Lucy's for lunch. It was another beautiful sunny day in Guangzhou, around 80 degrees, with a very slight breeze. We decided it was perfect weather to visit the park. After we were finished with lunch, we strolled through the beautiful park along the banks of the Pearl River.

The park was like nothing I'd ever seen. The grass was perfectly trimmed and the enormous old trees spread their branches out to create huge canopies. The palm trees swayed and the flowers nodded their heads in the breeze, keeping time with the music playing over the loud speakers. Chinese lanterns were strung in rows along the bank of the river. Dozens of boats sounded their horns as they rode the waves of the Pearl. Across the river were modern buildings that stood tall against the skyline. Marlee played and enjoyed the surroundings, and we used the beautiful setting to take pictures.

As we strolled back to the White Swan, we stopped in several of the shops along the way and admired the beautiful wares the vendors had to offer. I had heard that it was customary to barter with the shopkeepers, but the prices were so reasonable to begin with, I didn't feel the need to spend a lot of time trying to talk down their prices. Ever since the conversation I had had with Ivy back in Shenyang about incomes, I felt incredibly blessed for what I had and wanted to share some of it with the wonderful people of China. Just a few dollars didn't mean anything to me, but it meant the world to them.

We watched the clocks to make sure we were back at the hotel by 5:00 p.m. We were having a pizza party that night and had placed our orders for pizza earlier in the day. They were due to be delivered to our hotel rooms between 5:00 and 5:30. Just the thought of having pizza for dinner made my mouth water with anticipation. I had been craving pasta the entire trip, and although pizza wasn't pasta, it was still the closest thing to Italian food I had eaten in almost two weeks.

It made me almost feel like I was at home when the pizza deliveryman knocked on the door and handed us our pizza. The only thing that reminded me that we weren't in the States was the fact that he spoke no English and I paid him in Chinese yuan.

We took our pizza and the pop we had purchased at the store across the street and made our way downstairs to a large conference room on the first floor of the White Swan. The other families in our group soon arrived with their pizzas in one hand and their babies in the other.

There was a large playpen for the babies in the center of the room that reminded me of a World Wrestling Federation ring. The babies had a wonderful time playing while the parents sat and ate pizza and visited with each other. Marlee and Chloe played a game of tag with some of the older children in the group.

It was a nice, relaxing evening and the first chance I had to sit and talk with the parents since we received our babies. I compared historical notes with a couple of the moms and found that I wasn't alone in my years of infertility and medical frustration. Each family brought with them their own story that was unique, but we all had one thing in common—we longed for a child.

At the end of the evening, we all gave David our child's immunization record and money to pay for the doctor exam the next morning. I was amazed at how he could keep it all straight with so many families to take care of. He was genuinely a caring, loving man and it was apparent he dearly loved the children whom he was helping come to America.

ANOTHER DAY IN PARADISE

Our third day in Guangzhou was dedicated to preparing for the all-important interview with the American Consulate the following day. Immediately following breakfast, we all walked across the street from the White Swan to a little photo shop to have our daughters' pictures taken for their visa.

Most of the girls screamed when their parents sat them down for their photo, but Marlee sat quietly and did exactly as the photographer told her to do. The visa photo only required a side view from the shoulders up, so I was able to offer her support by kneeling in front of her and holding her hand.

After all the children had their turn in the photo studio, we gathered our children and backpacks and headed to the clinic for the doctor exam. Since the clinic was only eight blocks away and the weather was beautiful, we decided to walk. Marlee insisted on a piggyback, so I handed off my backpack and put her on instead. I was pretty sure they both weighed about the same. At this point in the trip, my back was so sore I walked hunched over anyway, so adding a three-year-old didn't seem to affect my posture.

The clinic was actually better than I had expected. Back in Shenyang, the Scotts had taken Chloe to the hospital for an ear infection. Upon their return, they told me how appalled they were at the unsanitary conditions of the hospital. Brenda was a nurse, so she saw things from a professional standpoint. I was fully expecting the same there in Guangzhou, but I was pleasantly surprised.

We had been told this clinic was approved by the American Consulate.

There was standing room only, however, as at least fifty families were jammed into the clinic to have their children examined. We were shown the four areas we were to go to, then told to split up into groups and go from one station to the next until we had completed them all.

The Scotts and I agreed that Chloe and Marlee should probably stay together so they could offer support to one another. They both looked around and instantly realized what was going on. Immediately they clasped hands and refused to let go of each other, which made it difficult to weigh them individually. We finally convinced them to let go for a few seconds, just long enough to let the nurse write down their height and weight. Marlee weighed in at 41 pounds and was 41 inches tall.

We continued to wade through the masses and complete all the examinations. The most difficult part was making our way through the crowd and waiting for our turn. Marlee was very cooperative as the doctors looked in her ears, down her throat, in her eyes, tested her reflexes, and examined her limbs and extremities. Once again, she didn't utter a peep. As long as Chloe was in sight, she was fine. In fact, she offered Chloe her bunny rabbit finger puppet to take in with her during one examination. As Chloe came out from behind the curtain, she gave it back to Marlee for her to take in with her. I was so touched by the care and concern these little girls had for each other.

We were in and out of the clinic in less than an hour and had until 3:00 p.m. to do as we pleased. Marlee and I met Elis back at the hotel room, then the three of us set out for an afternoon of power shopping. We started at Lucy's for lunch, then made our way down the streets of Shaymian Island to see what shops we hadn't yet explored.

Marlee had finally learned her store etiquette, so shopping was much more pleasurable. Actually, she had learned how to completely suck up to every shop attendant and had each of them waiting on her hand and foot.

In one little shop, a very sweet young lady asked if she could take care of my daughter while I shopped. I said that would be fine and Marlee took her hand and went off to play. Elis and I took advantage of the time and enjoyed shopping without help from a three year old.

At one point I looked toward the back of the shop to see how Marlee was doing. She was sitting on a stool at a beautiful little coffee table. Across from her, sitting on his own stool, was the store owner, a gentleman at least in his sixties. He had made tea for Marlee, peeled an orange, and was showing her how to shell peanuts. I smiled when I saw the care this man was showing Marlee. He glanced up at me and gave me the, "She's okay mama, don't worry" look.

When I was done with my shopping, I had to coax Marlee away. They had showered her with so much attention that she didn't want to leave. They gave me a handful of candy to put in my pocket for later, handed Marlee an orange to take with her, and even posed for some pictures. I thanked them many times for their

kindness and generosity. I assured them we would

probably be back to finish our gift list.

The afternoon went all too quickly as we lost ourselves in the charming shops. Before we knew it, it was time to get back to the hotel to start working on the paperwork for the U.S. Consulate interview. Marlee and I left Elis to enjoy an afternoon of peace and quiet on her own.

Back at the White Swan, I ran into Brenda Scott who offered to take the girls swimming at the pool while I worked on my papers. Marlee was more than happy to go, as she and Chloe hadn't spent much time together since we'd arrived in Guangzhou. We had agreed that we should wean the girls from each other gradually in preparation for the final good-bye that was eminent.

I took my large folder of papers up to the Bohan family's room on the 21st floor where we had agreed to meet. They had a large suite, which made it more comfortable for us to spread out and do our paperwork. David took us through each document line by line, giving us explicit instructions on how to answer each question. All these documents would be presented to the U.S. Consulate at our interview the next morning, so everything had to be exactly right. Nearly three hours later, we finished filling out all the forms. We were exhausted!

It was dinnertime and we were starving. David suggested a very good Chinese restaurant just down the street and many of us agreed it would be fun to try something besides Lucy's for dinner. We had eaten American food practically the entire time we'd been in Guangzhou, so we were ready for some authentic Chinese food again.

I accompanied Clyde Scott back to his room to pick up Marlee. She and Chloe had had a wonderful time playing all afternoon and Brenda said that Marlee loved the pool. But even after spending several hours together, the girls still cried when we said good-bye. I cringed as I thought to myself what it was going to be like when they would have to say their final farewell.

Marlee and I stopped by our room to pick up Elis, then met several of the other families for dinner. It was an enchanting night in Guangzhou. We guessed the weather to be about 75 degrees with a very slight breeze. The sun was starting to set over the beautiful Pearl River and it cast a wonderful hue over the city. We strolled down the bustling sidewalk in search of the restaurant David had recommended. We stepped inside the lobby and saw dozens of tanks that obviously held our choice of dinner.

The smell was less than intriguing, and the sight of the snakes, frogs, and unidentified swimming things curbed our appetites. We all looked at each other, winced, and simultaneously said, "Let's go to Lucy's."

So once again, we enjoyed a wonderful American meal at Lucy's, our new home away from home. We talked and visited until almost 9:00 p.m. Tom Bohan entertained us with his story of their lunch that day that consisted of dog and poisonous snake. We were laughing so hard we had tears streaming down our faces.

When we realized how late the hour was, we hurried back to the hotel to get a good night's sleep. We wanted to be rested and fresh for our all-important interview at the Consulate the next morning.

THE INTERVIEW

I must have checked my alarm a dozen times before I went to sleep, but I still woke up before it rang. I was shaking with anticipation of the consulate interview. David reiterated to us the importance of being on time. I intentionally planned extra time in the morning to go over my documents I had prepared the day before to make sure they were in order. There were seventeen total, all to be presented in a specific order.

I woke Marlee and got her ready for the interview. I had purchased a cute little denim jumper for her the previous day. She was none too happy about wearing it and kept trying to pull it down over her legs. I realized that she had probably never worn a dress before and that it was somewhat disconcerting to her. I lifted her up to look in the mirror and both Elis and I made a fuss over how cute she looked. I added blue daisy hair clips to her sleek, black hair and finished off the outfit with white tights and white shoes. She still resisted, but I ignored her obvious dislike for her outfit and escorted her out the door for breakfast.

Although we had the feast of a king laid out in front of us, it was hard to eat. My stomach churned with nervousness. I kept looking at my watch and prodding Marlee to eat so we wouldn't be late. Our appointment at the Consulate was at 9:30. We were to meet David at 9:15 in the lobby, then walk over to the Consulate together as a group. The Consulate was located on the same block as the White Swan Hotel, therefore it would only be a short walk.

There were four families whose appointments were at the same time as ours. Three of the families arrived several minutes early and we visited while we waited for the fourth family. At 9:20 we started to get nervous when the fourth family hadn't arrived yet.

Maggie had met us rather than David, and we prodded her to just leave with us rather than risk being late. She said we could wait another few minutes and then we would have to go. If we did not appear on time for our appointments, they would be canceled and our daughters would not get their visas to leave China.

Finally at 9:25, Maggie said we couldn't wait any longer and we started down the hall towards the exit of the White Swan. As we rounded the corner to leave the hotel, the final family came hurrying and apologized for being late. I tried not to let my demeanor show how panicked I was, but I was afraid it was apparent. I said something to the effect of, "No time for apologies, we have to hurry," as I scooped up Marlee and started to run.

Clyde had gathered Chloe up into his arms as well, since we didn't have time to wait for three-year-old legs to keep up. The girls insisted on holding hands, however, so Clyde and I trotted closely along side each other as Marlee and Chloe clutched each other.

I was relieved to find it was only about two blocks to the Consulate. It was apparent we had reached our destination when we came upon a crowd so large it filled the entire street. There were hundreds of people waiting outside the U.S. Consulate.

Maggie took us to the front of the crowd and we waited to enter. There were armed guards outside the tall black gates. Marlee and Chloe found a tree surrounded by a brick circle that they wanted to walk on. It was apparent it would be several minutes before our turn to enter, so I let the girls play. A guard watched them curiously and I wasn't sure if he was suspicious or entertained. I smiled at him to let him know the girls were just playing, but got no response from his stoic face.

Suddenly I heard someone in our group say, "Here we go!" We gathered the girls and stepped inside the tiny entry. It was only big enough for one person at a time, and we had to coax Marlee and Chloe to let go of each other's hand.

There were two uniformed men who stood on either side of a metal detector. We gave them our papers and backpacks to search as we walked through the detector. They searched everything thoroughly before we were allowed to enter. The girls had to wait for each other, of course, which created quite a jam in the tiny little building. Finally we were all cleared and proceeded across a courtyard to the front doors of the U.S. Consulate.

Another checkpoint just inside the door required us to show our passports. We were allowed through the doors one at a time and escorted down long narrow halls, up stairs, and finally into a waiting room. Maggie instructed us to wait there until our name was called. I was so nervous, I was afraid I was going to wet my pants. Fortunately, there was a restroom there in the waiting area, which we all took turns using. It was comforting to know I wasn't the only one nervous beyond belief.

Chloe and Marlee got out the finger puppets and started to play on the floor. We sat on the benches, facing each other in a square, nervously making small talk. After about ten minutes, they called our names. I quickly gathered the puppets off the floor and took Marlee by the hand.

We walked into a room roughly the size of a typical living room. There were four desks lined up in a row facing us. A U.S. Consulate official sat at each desk. The room was filled to capacity with families waiting for their interviews. We seated ourselves on the benches across the room facing the interview desks. Occasionally a family name would be called and they would seat themselves in the chairs in front of the interviewers.

I heard the name "Turner" shouted out above the loud crowd. I looked up and saw a lady motion with her hand which desk I was to go to. I gathered Marlee and made my way through the crowded room to the desk across the room. I sat down and put Marlee on the chair beside me. She immediately indicated she wanted to sit on my lap, so I settled her on my legs as I retrieved my paperwork from the file folder I carried with me.

I handed my stack of papers to the young woman and she began to file through them, occasionally stamping and signing. I sat nervously with Marlee still on my lap. She continued to look back over her shoulder at Chloe and wanted to go play with her. The Consulate worker told me that would be okay, so I let her go. I was a little more relaxed not having to figure out ways to entertain Marlee.

We continued the paperwork, but at one point the woman flipped back and forth between the same two pages. It was apparent she had found some sort of discrepancy. She left the desk a couple times to show the papers to another Consulate worker. Finally, she came back to the desk and told me she had found an error in

Marlee's Abandonment Certificate and it would have to be re-translated.

Panic raced through my body as I envisioned having to get on an airplane and fly back to Shenyang to have it corrected. The woman hailed the attention of David and explained the situation to him. David saw the alarm in my eyes, put his hand on my shoulder, and said, "Don't worry. It's just a minor mistake. We can fix it downstairs." He took the document from me, along with 100 yuan to pay for the re-translation, and told me not to worry. The Consulate worker finished her paperwork, asked for my last three year's tax statements, then put all the papers in a large folder and told me to wait again until my name was called.

I joined Marlee back on the benches where she was playing with Chloe and told Clyde and Brenda about what had happened. I didn't have much time to fret over the situation, however. My name was called again, and Marlee and I made our way down to the other end of the room to the final desk. Just as we heard our name, the Scott's name was called also. Coincidentally, they were seated at the desk just beside us. The girls once again insisted on holding hands, so Chloe sat on Brenda's lap, while Marlee climbed up into Clyde's lap in order to reach her best friend.

My interviewer had an inquisitive look about her as all this was taking place, so I explained to her the circumstances and how these best friends couldn't stand to be apart from each other. She thought it was very sweet and wondered aloud to me what would happen when they had to separate for good. I told her I didn't want to think about it and would cross that bridge when we came to it.

The interviewer looked through all my papers, saw that everything was in order, and had me raise my right hand. I swore that all the information was true and correct and that I would love and raise Marlee to the best of my ability and never abandon her. I handed her Marlee's two visa pictures and that was that. It was over and done with. She congratulated me and wished us well. I instantly felt as if a huge weight had been lifted from my shoulders.

Marlee and I left the U.S. Consulate building, stopping outside the gates to take a couple photographs to document the occasion. The same guard eyed us just as he had before. I smiled, waved at him, then thanked him for the hospitality the Consulate had shown us. A tiny little

smiled graced his lips, and that was all.

NEW LIFE CELEBRATION

All the families met that evening to join together in a "New Life Celebration Party." We used the beautiful backdrop of the White Swan lobby to take several group photos. Surprisingly, all the children and babies seemed to be on their best behavior for the pictures. There was a feeling of comfort in the air having completed the interview with the Consulate. We were all ready to let down our hair and celebrate the amazing task we had just completed.

We drove through the beautiful streets of Guangzhou at sunset. The nightlife was just beginning. Thousands of people filled the streets, dressed up and ready for a night of partying. We passed by dozens of clubs and restaurants, all very ornate and elegant. I wished to myself that I had a month to spend in this enchanting city to explore its treasures and culture.

I glanced down to the seat beside me where Marlee was sitting. She was fast asleep, her head still upright against the back of the seat. Her left arm was stretched across the aisle of the bus, grasping the hand of Chloe, who was in the seat directly across from her. She too was snoring peacefully. I called this adorable scene to the attention of everyone on the bus and handed my camera back for someone to take a photo. They were all touched by the love these two little girls shared for each other and they reiterated again how difficult it was going to be for them to leave each other. I realized that moment was now only two days away, and I was going to have to face it whether I wanted to or not.

The buses pulled up in front of a very beautiful, modern building. The girls' eyes fluttered open when the bus came to a stop. We exited onto a red carpet that led to glass doors held open by uniformed valets.

The spacious lobby inside was filled with the sound of Vivaldi being played by a live chamber orchestra. We stood and listened to the music until the piece ended. The girls were quite captivated by the instruments and the sound that flowed like a peaceful running stream. I took Marlee over to where the cellists played and tried to explain to her that I played the cello, but it was apparent she didn't understand what I was saying.

The music ended, the audience applauded, and we proceeded down the beautiful marble stairs to the lower level of the shopping center. We passed posh designer boutiques along the way, and commented on the very fine merchandise in the windows. I had never seen such an ornate shopping mall, even in the States. We finally came to the end of the hall and entered the Hard Rock Café, Guangzhou.

The employees greeted us with open arms. They led us to a special area they had set up just for our party. There were three long tables with highchairs scattered intermittently. On each high chair were balloons, a stuffed dinosaur, and crayons. Marlee and Chloe were still hanging on to each other; therefore, we had to rearrange the chairs and sitting arrangements in order for them to be together.

Chloe fit very nicely into her highchair, but I struggled to get Marlee's long legs into her seat. She looked at me in disgust as I tried every way I could think of to get her into the highchair. I was going to just put her in a chair to sit for dinner, but she insisted on having a chair like Chloe's. Finally, one of the Hard Rock employees came along and helped me by taking off the tray of the high chair.

Chloe and Marlee colored their children's menus and entertained each other with their dinosaurs and balloons while we waited for our dinner.

Marlee didn't seem very hungry, as she kept feeding her dinner to Chloe. That was my first indication that perhaps she wasn't feeling well. I had never seen my daughter pass up food. She'd had a runny nose for a couple days, but I just passed it off as a reaction to the temperature change from Shenyang to Guangzhou. Elis and I had been feeling a bit congested as well.

After dinner, the Great Wall guides, David, Maggie and Jeanne, gave each adopted child a beautiful red Chinese paper lantern. They lit a candle inside, then let the children carry their lanterns. I turned around to see Marlee and Chloe walking side by side, carrying their glowing lanterns at the end of a stick. When I realized there was a burning candle inside, I ran to their side to make sure they didn't light the Hard Rock Café on fire. I was pretty sure that wouldn't leave a good impression.

After several minutes, I became much too anxious about the burning candles in the paper lanterns, so I blew out the flame and suggested to Marlee we go dance. The band had just started and several other families were already out on the dance floor. Marlee wouldn't dance without her life partner to date, so I held Marlee and Clyde held Chloe as we danced beside each other.

Marlee and I spent over an hour dancing, singing, and taking pictures. All the families enjoyed the music that was provided by a Caribbean band, and took turns dancing with each other. We swapped children and partners, danced with the guides, and even danced by ourselves when we couldn't find a partner. The entire restaurant was one big love-fest that evening.

Marlee was unusually clingy that evening, and insisted that I carry her constantly. She had a total meltdown if I was out of her sight. She seemed to be quite warm, so I took off her sweater and tried to cool her down. She acted like a little girl who was getting sick, but I told myself she was just tired from all the activities.

Nine o'clock rolled around and we were all partied out. It had been an incredibly long day. We gathered our children, purchased the obligatory Hard Rock Café t-shirts, and loaded the bus for the hotel. Marlee lay in my arms with her head on my chest and fell asleep within minutes.

We arrived back at the White Swan, and I carried her to our room and put her in bed. Elis and I were exhausted from our busy day, so we also crawled into our "Hard Rock" beds and drifted off to sleep.

FOR BETTER OR WORSE

I had an indication that I was in for stormy weather when my daughter woke up every half-hour during the night crying. She would scream uncontrollably, cough until I thought she was going to choke, then suddenly fall back asleep. We went through this ritual the whole night; then Marlee finally woke up at 6:00 a.m. It was Valentine's Day and our last day in Guangzhou.

She got out of her bed and walked around the room aimlessly, whimpering and lethargic. She walked over to me, crying, then suddenly fell face-first onto her bed, sound asleep. She slept for a short time, then woke up and repeated the same behavior. Her face was red, her cheeks on fire, and I could tell she had a raging temperature. She almost acted as if she was hallucinating.

I dug out the children's Motrin I had brought along and Elis and I tried to wrestle Marlee down to give it to her. I squirted the grape-flavored medicine into her mouth and prayed that it would do the trick. She immediately sat up, looked at me in disgust, and spit the entire mouthful of medicine into my lap.

Since my precious daughter wouldn't take her medicine, I decided that perhaps a bath would cool her down. I filled the tub with warm water, stripped us both down, and sat in the bath with Marlee on my lap. I had cool water slowly drizzling from the faucet to slowly lower the temperature of the water.

After about thirty minutes, she seemed to be cooler and a little more coherent. I wrapped her in a towel and sat with her on the bed singing songs. She fell asleep in my arms. But as I tried to lay her down, she woke up screaming again.

I looked at Elis and said, "What should I do? Should I take her to the doctor?" Elis, with her wisdom in being one of seven children, said that she thought I probably should. She quickly packed a bag for me and I carried Marlee, still in her pajamas, to the elevator. The ever-present hall monitor immediately recognized the panic on my face and explained to me how to find the hotel clinic on the third floor.

Although everything was written in Chinese, I recognized the clinic by the big red and white cross on the door. Marlee had fallen asleep again, and I juggled my extremely heavy daughter to push the ringer on the door. The door opened within seconds, and a very pleasant-looking lady in a white coat escorted me in. I started to explain to her my situation, when she shook her head and motioned with her hand for me to wait.

She disappeared around the corner and appeared with another woman, who said very sweetly, "How can we help you?" I told them about Marlee's condition, then waited on a long green plastic couch that had been preserved from the 1950's. Marlee still slept in my arms, but would occasionally whimper. After just a few moments, I was escorted behind the curtain that separated the waiting area from the exam room.

A pleasant middle-aged woman sat behind a desk, greeted me, and asked me to sit in the chair beside her. The interpreter explained Marlee's symptoms to her, and she nodded. She asked a few questions about her name and age, then started to examine her while she was still in my arms. The stethoscope on Marlee's chest woke her up, and she started to cry and flail around listlessly. I reassured her and kissed her on the cheek. After just a few minutes, she suddenly fell fast asleep, limp in my arms. The doctor looked at me in surprise, then asked if that's how she had been acting all morning. I nodded my head and shrugged my shoulders in bewilderment.

The doctor talked to Marlee and tried to get her to wake up. She spoke in Chinese, and Marlee's eyes slowly opened and focused on the doctor and what she was saying. She opened her mouth as the doctor asked her to, stuck out her tongue, and let the doctor put the tongue depressor in her mouth without even as much as a gag. No sooner had Marlee said, "Aahhh" when the doctor's eyes widened. Her eyebrows scrunched together and her head pulled back as she exclaimed, "Ohhhh, very big!"

I looked at the nurse who was interpreting, and she explained to me that Marlee's tonsils were very enlarged. They would need to give her a treatment for her throat, then administer an antibiotic through an IV. I asked how long it would take, and the nurse told me about two hours. Two hours! I remembered my daughter spitting out her Motrin in my lap, and could only envision the chaos she would create when they put a needle in her arm for two hours. I really had no choice, however, and agreed to do whatever it took to make Marlee feel better.

A nurse brought me a form to sign authorizing her treatment, and explained that it would be very expensive, about $100. Fortunately, I still had plenty of money left and asked them if I could pay them in U.S. currency rather than Chinese yuan. They nodded their heads and we began the treatment.

The doctor disappeared to the back room and appeared with an apparatus that looked like a humidifier with a large hose attached. They explained that Marlee would breathe through the tube and the medicine would help her throat. I held her in my lap as she clutched her pink blanket and the doctor placed the breathing tube in her throat. She was still asleep, but they spoke to her in Chinese and explained what they were doing.

Within just a few minutes, Marlee's eyes opened, she sat up, and wrapped her hands around the tube. It must have felt good on her throat, because she inhaled deeply and held it tightly to her mouth. After thirty minutes, they shut off the breathing machine and explained to Marlee they were going to give her some medicine by putting it in her arm.

I carried her over to a bed on the other side of the room and helped her lie down and get comfortable. Marlee cooperated completely in preparing her arm. I told myself this was the calm before the storm and geared myself up for quite a scene. The nurse slid the needle into her arm, secured it with tape, and set the drip, all without even a single flinch from my daughter. She didn't whimper, resist, or even ask what they were doing. I pulled up a rolling stool and tried to get comfortable. I knew it was going to be a long morning.

For the first hour, Marlee remained motionless on the bed, occasionally looking at me, and then closing her eyes. I stroked her hair and kissed her cheek a thousand times. Finally, I couldn't hold back the tears any longer. I was worried, exhausted, and frightened. Since I had gotten very little sleep the night before, I desperately wanted to find just a few minutes to close my eyes and rest. I kept trying to lay my head beside hers on her pillow, but Marlee adamantly insisted that I not.

Midway through the IV, she started to become more alert, talking and interacting with me. She was becoming restless, and we still had an hour to go. Time seems to stand still when you're trying to entertain a three-year-old who has a needle in her arm. I pulled out the ever-entertaining finger puppets and we played with them until my imagination was tapped out. Then I sang to her until my throat was sore.

Marlee soon complained that she was hungry, which I didn't doubt. After all, she had eaten very little the day before. I was pretty hungry myself, since it was after 11:00 a.m. and we'd been up for five hours with nothing to eat. The doctor told me I could go get her something to eat and they would keep watch over her. I explained to Marlee that I would be right back with food for her and hesitantly left her lying on the bed in the clinic.

I hurried to our hotel room as quickly as I could. I found some fruit snacks, cheerios, and a banana, and then grabbed a water bottle from the refrigerator. I was back in the clinic in just a matter of minutes. The doctor made me show her what I had brought, and she shook her head at everything I had. She said that Marlee had a case of indigestion and that those foods would irritate her stomach. I suggested a few other things, and she shook her head at those as well.

I was incredibly frustrated at this point and equally as exhausted, so my natural reaction took over and I started to cry. I told the nurse I didn't know what the doctor wanted me to feed her. The doctor sighed heavily in what

I interpreted to be an indication of frustration with me. She went to her office and came out with a box of crackers. She handed me a package and told me to feed them to my daughter.

Marlee devoured the crackers as quickly as I could feed them to her, alternating with sips of water. I was on the edge of passing out from lack of food myself, so I tore open her fruit snacks and snuck them in my mouth when Marlee wasn't looking. I should have known I couldn't pull anything over on my bright daughter, however, and she insisted that I share the fruit snacks with her. I glanced around to see if the doctor or nurses were watching, then quickly popped one into her mouth and held my finger up to my mouth to let her know she shouldn't let the doctor see what she was eating. She smiled at me as she slyly popped another one in her mouth.

By this time, Marlee was very congenial and carrying on lengthy conversations with the nurses in Chinese. I anxiously watched the clock hands move to 11:30 a.m. It was finally time to take the IV out of her arm. Once again, Marlee didn't even flinch when they removed the needle and put on the band-aid. They all commented on what a good patient she had been.

The doctor explained to me that she wanted Marlee to come back at 4:00 that afternoon for another IV. The words were like shock waves through my body. Again? I couldn't believe they were going to make her do it all over again. I asked if it would take another two hours, and they said it would only be about twenty minutes this time. I also inquired about additional cost and was happy to find out that the second treatment was included in the price.

I gathered my exhausted daughter into my tired arms and followed the nurse back behind the curtain to the reception desk. She gave me a bottle of cough syrup and several packets of Ceclor, an antibiotic powder that could be mixed with water. She gave me instructions on how to dispense it to Marlee and suggested that I take her to our own family doctor once we arrived home in the States.

I explained to the nurses that Marlee refused to take medication, so they both spoke with her at length and told her she should take her medicine so she would feel better. I smiled when I saw her cross her arms and shake her head in response to the nurses' pleas.

We walked out of the clinic four hours after we arrived, holding two medications, a receipt for $113, and

an appointment card to return at 4:30 that afternoon.
Marlee wrapped her long pink long-john covered legs
around my waist and put her head on my shoulder. I
carried her to the elevators and waited for a car to take us
back to the 11th floor. Several people in the elevator
sympathized with both of us over our ordeal, as it was
obvious we had both been through the ringer that
morning. Neither of us looked very perky.

I rang the bell of our hotel room, hoping Elis would
answer. My hands were full of a sleeping little girl and I
couldn't reach my room key that was in my fanny pack.
Fortunately, she had already returned from the morning
of touring and opened the door for us. I was disappointed
that Marlee and I had missed the activities planned for
the morning, a visit to Guangzhou's largest kindergarten.

But I had instructed Elis to take a lot of pictures and I would have copies made.

Marlee woke up as I tried to lay her down on the bed. She again complained that she was hungry. Elis and I put our heads together to think of something that would be kind to her sensitive stomach and fill her up. Elis suggested a bowl of congi, a disgusting looking rice-type hot mush. Marlee had devoured it every time I'd given it to her. The hotel didn't have it on the room service menu, but when I called the kitchen, they suggested I go down to the dining room to purchase it.

Elis kept watch over Marlee while I went down to get her food. She knew I needed a break from my sick daughter and I thanked her for that. But evidently the dining room had to send someone by bicycle to the rice paddy to harvest the rice, because I waited for what seemed like eternity for a simple bowl of congi. I finally returned to my starving child and she inhaled the large bowl of rice in a matter of minutes.

It was closing in on 1:00 p.m. and our appointment at the U.S. Consulate to pick up Marlee's visa was at 3:00. She was so tired she could hardly keep her eyes open. I laid down with her on her bed and she was asleep before her head hit the pillow. Elis and I took advantage of the quiet, dark room and slept for an hour before we had to get ready for the visa appointment. Even my rock-hard bed didn't hinder my sleep for that hour.

HAVE VISA, WILL TRAVEL

After only an hour of sleep, my obnoxious alarm went off. I quietly slipped out of bed and into the bathroom to attempt a presentable look for the U.S. Consulate. Today's visa presentation was somewhat extraordinary in that Mike Marine, a U.S. official, was in town on business and asked to personally present the children with their visas. Mr. Marine and his wife were the first Americans to adopt a child from China twenty years previously.

I dressed in an authentic Chinese silk blouse and black dress pants. After covering the dark circles under my eyes with make-up and splashing on some blush and lipstick, I figured that was as good as it was going to get.

I let Marlee sleep until the very last moment before I woke her. I dressed her in the beautiful black and red outfit I had bought in Shenyang. We topped her ensemble with a black velvet hat and she looked absolutely adorable. Once she shook the cobwebs out of her head, she was fairly congenial considering all she'd been through that day.

Because the conference room at the U.S. Consulate was small, they limited the number of people at the Visa ceremony. Only the immediate family was allowed to attend, so we left Elis at the hotel to start her packing for our long trip home the next day. The other families had gathered at the famous "red couch" in the White Swan lobby. Everyone inquired about Marlee's health and said they had missed us that morning.

The weather was somewhat blustery that day, to coin a phrase from Pooh. The temperature was fifty degrees at best and the wind was so strong it was hard to walk. We made the short journey to the U.S. Consulate and proceeded through the same security checks as before.

Our guides escorted us to a meeting room set up with about a hundred chairs and a podium at the front. The Consulate officials called out our names and instructed us where to sit. Unfortunately, the Scott family was seated in another section, so Marlee and Chloe weren't able to sit together.

Marlee promptly stood on her chair and shouted to Chloe from across the room. I tried to make her understand she needed to be quiet and attempted to entertain her with her puppets. As I reached down to grab some fruit snacks out of her bag, she slipped out of her chair and took off down the isle toward Chloe. She had her finger puppets in hand and ignored my calls for her to return.

Just then, a procession of U.S. Consulate officials entered and walked to the front of the room. Applause started and I looked down the long isle of chairs to where Marlee was sitting on Clyde's lap. He caught my eye, nodded, and put Marlee down and instructed her to come back to me. She smiled at me as she climbed up on my lap and made me understand that she had to give her puppets to Chloe so she would have something to play with.

The ceremony was very conducive to a room full of fussing children. Mr. Marine spoke for only about five minutes, then proceeded with the presentation of the visas. He called about five families at a time to come to the front of the room one by one and receive their visa.

He shook each parent's hand and acknowledged each child. Then the families all stood in a line with Mr. Marine so photos could be taken. This ritual was repeated until each family had come to the front. I guessed there to be about forty-five families in all that day.

The ceremony followed with a reception of punch and cookies. Several U.S. Consulate officials approached me and congratulated both Marlee and me. I was struggling to balance punch, cookies, my extremely valuable visa packet, and a squirming three-year-old. The three-year-old won the battle, so to speak, and my punch went flying. Most of it landed on the floor, fortunately, but a few drops grazed my pants and the visa packet I was holding.

Several Consulate officials saw my predicament and rushed to assist me. I must have looked pretty pathetic.

They helped me pick up all my things that fell to the floor, asked if I needed any more assistance, and cautioned me to take special care of the visa packet. I was tired and frustrated and wanted to say, "What do you think I am, a moron? Of course I know I'm supposed to take care of the visa!" But instead, I smiled graciously and thanked them for their assistance. I explained how I was traveling without my husband and that I needed a few more arms to hang on to everything.

Marlee seemed to be feeling much better and was back to her usual challenging self. I needed to get out of that crowded room into some fresh air, and Marlee needed to exhaust some energy. She and I walked back to the White Swan against the cool wind. It was almost 4:30 p.m. and we had to get back to the clinic for her second round of antibiotics.

Once again, my daughter was the perfect patient and sat perfectly still for the twenty minutes it took to administer the IV. The staff at the clinic wished us luck in our journey home and sent Marlee off with hugs and kisses.

We spent the afternoon organizing and packing for our long trip home the next day. We were amazed at the amount of stuff we had accumulated in thirteen days. I quickly realized there was no physical way I was going to be able to put all my things in the suitcase and duffle bag I had brought with me.

We made a quick trip cross the street to Jennifer's, a little shop that sold suitcases in addition to hundreds of souvenirs. I found a large suitcase on wheels, close to the size of the one I had, for only $22. We figured that would do the trick to get all of our wonderful Chinese purchases safely back to the States.

We'd been packing for over two hours when our stomachs reminded us it was time to take a dinner break. We called Terry and Laura Biggs, another family in our group, to see if they wanted to join us for dinner. They were also packing for the trip and said they'd love to join us.

None of us were in the mood to walk very far since we'd had a very long, exhausting day and needed to get to bed early to catch our early morning flight to Hong Kong. We opted to try the hotel restaurants since there were several to choose from.

What we didn't take into account, however, was the fact that it was Valentine's Day. We soon discovered that it was quite an event in China, and every restaurant in the hotel was full. After almost an hour of being turned away from every restaurant we could find, Laura suggested we try the noodle bar outside the White Swan. She said that the atmosphere wasn't much to look at, but the food was good and cheap.

I couldn't believe I'd been in Guangzhou five days and there was a restaurant on the block I hadn't yet discovered. When Laura pointed it out though, I saw how I easily bypassed it. It was adjacent to a dry cleaning store and it had no sign indicating it was a restaurant.

Laura was certainly right. The atmosphere left much to be desired. It was a tiny, claustrophobic little place. There were approximately ten tables in the entire restaurant. It wasn't incredibly clean, but it wasn't so dirty that it made me nervous to eat there. As hungry as I was, I think my standards had lowered considerably; I was feeling game for anything they put in front of me. It seemed like eternity since our trip to the doctor that morning.

We waited for quite some time before Terry finally motioned with his hand and caught the attention of a waitress. She had been standing behind the counter since we'd entered the restaurant, yet didn't acknowledge us at all. She spoke no English, so we simply pointed to the item on the menu and she nodded her head. Fortunately, we all ordered the same thing. Terry and Laura had tried it previously and said it was very good. Elis and I were too tired to make a decision on our own, so we agreed with their recommendation. We ordered six plates of noodles with vegetables and chicken and six glasses of lemon-lime soda.

In just a few minutes, they brought our food out to us. The plates were the size of platters, and the noodles were piled at least three inches high. I don't know if the food was really as fantastic as I thought it was, or if it was just the incredible satisfaction I felt to finally curb the gnawing hunger in my stomach.

The bill for the entire meal, all six plates of food and the drinks, came to 70 yuan, which converted to a little less than $8. I wished I had discovered this little place early in the week. It was close to the hotel, the food was delicious and it would have saved me a lot of money. Still, it didn't have the ambiance of Lucy's. In fact, it had no ambiance at all.

We finished every last noodle on our platters, then realized it was after 8:00 p.m. The bus for the airport was leaving promptly at 6:00 the next morning; therefore, our alarms would have to be set for the horrid hour of 4:00 a.m. We said our goodnights and adjourned to our rooms to finish the huge task of packing.

My precious daughter kicked into overdrive that evening, and I was beginning to wonder if perhaps there was a little something extra slipped into her IV that day. She danced around the hotel room in her pink long-johns singing, jumping, making up words, and playing hide-and-seek.

She made packing a challenge with her games. I couldn't figure out why I was finding peanut shells scattered among my things, then discovered out of the corner of my eye that Marlee was quietly slipping the shells of the peanuts she was eating into my suitcase. Occasionally I would turn around to find the item I had just placed in my suitcase missing, and Marlee was standing with it hidden behind her back.

Her antics escalated the later it got. Our bags were to be packed and waiting outside our door by 10:00 p.m. With only fifteen minutes left, I frantically stuffed things into the bags and didn't care how organized it was at that point. I was pretty close to stuffing my daughter in one of those bags as well. If she hadn't been so darn cute, I would have. She had made up a song and dance that had us laughing uncontrollably.

I interrupted my packing several times to catch her theatrics on video. It was prime material to archive for when she was sixteen and her prom date came to pick her up. The lyrics of her original song consisted of, "Ah so, ah so, ah so so so!" Her hips swiveled back and forth in sync with her arms, somewhat like "The Twist." Her song had consistent rhythm and lyrics, but the choreography varied depending on what she was feeling at the moment, somewhat of an interpretive dance. She had to occasionally stop and pop a peanut into her mouth in a freeze frame mode, and then suddenly burst back into song and dance after she had chewed it. Each time the volume was louder.

The bags were packed and waiting in the hall, our carry-on luggage was ready, our pajamas were on, the beds were turned down, and Marlee was still bouncing off the walls. Every time I would put her in her bed, she would jump up and start singing and gyrating around the room again.

At 11:00 p.m. I finally turned off the lights, put Marlee in her bed and insisted she go to sleep. It was hard to tell her that with a stern demeanor because she'd had me laughing for the last two hours. The last thing I heard before I fell asleep was her quiet echo of, "Ah so, ah so, ah so so so."

THE JOURNEY HOME

I sat up suddenly in my bed, panic racing through my body. I had just emerged from a dream where I was on the airplane home and Marlee was hysterical. I couldn't calm her down, everyone on the plane was staring at me, and I was as emotionally desperate as I had ever felt.

I shook my head and realized I was still in my bed. I breathed a sigh of relief that it was only a dream, and then had the overwhelming feeling of de ja vu. I thought to myself, "I knew it was going to be like this. I knew the trip home would be horrible." But I slipped into my comfortable denial zone and told myself it was only a dream; everything would be fine.

At 4:00 a.m. the alarm triggered the incredibly nervous pit in my stomach. I stumbled into the shower and spent the next few minutes letting the water splash onto my face in hopes it would wake me into consciousness. I prayed that I would have the strength to endure the long journey ahead of us. I had had less than eight hours sleep in the last two nights combined, and knew it would be at least thirty hours until I could go to bed again.

I woke Marlee at 5:15 a.m. and dressed her while she was still groggy. She looked at me as if I was trying to torture her and kept rolling over in an attempt to go back to sleep. I said, "Well, that's what you get when you stay up partying all night." I knew she didn't understand a word I said and I laughed at myself for even saying it. But I felt somewhat vindicated having the opportunity to say that as I thought of all the times during my teenage years when my dad said to me, "The dancer has to pay the fiddler."

I scooped my irritated, sleepy daughter into my arms and we slipped quietly out the door to the elevator with our bags in hand. The always-present hall monitor helped us to the elevator and pushed the button for us one last time.

The only people at the breakfast buffet were the families from Great Wall who were leaving that morning. It was still dark outside. All we could see of the beautiful Pearl River outside the window of the dining room was the waves illuminated by moonbeams.

Marlee refused to eat any breakfast. In fact, she was somewhat combative. I grabbed a couple of bananas and some finger food and stuffed them into my backpack for later. I knew she'd be hungry soon and would be as grumpy as a bear because of it.

I tried to persuade her to follow me out of the restaurant, but she promptly responded by throwing herself on the floor screaming. With my twenty-pound backpack on my back and a large duffle bag over my shoulder, I wrestled my grumpy daughter into my arms and carried her kicking and screaming to the White Swan lobby to check out.

All the families quietly boarded the buses as the sunrise woke up the city. Marlee put her head in my lap and dozed quietly as we drove for the final time through the streets of Guangzhou. I closed my eyes also and savored every moment I had to relax.

The thirty-minute drive came to an end all too quickly as the bus pulled up in front of the Guangzhou airport.

Elis found a luggage cart and we struggled to load our four large suitcases and three carry-ons.

We maneuvered through the sea of people in the airport lobby, following David to the check-in area. After handing us our boarding passes, we said our good-byes to him and thanked him for all his help during our stay. He waved good-bye to us as he sent us through the security area.

We walked through a myriad of checkpoints, x-ray machines, and passport checks. Each time we had to unload our entire assortment of luggage, then load it back up again. Finally, after the third time I unloaded the heavy suitcases off the cart, they went on to the conveyor belt and were off to our airplane.

Our final stop was to fill out departure cards since we were leaving Mainland China and going to Hong Kong. I stood in line for twenty minutes with Marlee wailing at my feet. She had taken off running and I had to leave the line to chase her down and bring her back kicking and screaming. We'd been battling each other from the moment she woke up that morning.

When it was finally my turn to show all my documentation to the airport official, he looked at my departure card, scowled, and tossed it back to me as he said, "No pencil!" I couldn't find a pen to fill out the card, so I had used a small pencil that was on the counter with the cards.

Marlee was screaming at my feet and I was exhausted. Hearing the words, "No pencil" put me over the edge. I grabbed my papers, picked up my carry-on luggage, and flung it as far as I possibly could. I felt like I was having a nervous breakdown right there in front of our entire group.

I felt a hand on my shoulder and I turned to see who was witnessing my tantrum. It was Debbie, one of the moms in our group, who was from New York. She said, "I know you're frustrated Shannon. Just take a deep breath and calm down. Everything's going to be okay."

I thanked her for her support and wiped the tears from my eyes, then proceeded back to the counter to fill out another departure card, this time in pen.

As I approached the long line again, it parted as if it were the Red Sea. Everyone motioned for me to go to the front of the line. I guessed it was probably because they didn't want to witness another meltdown by me or listen to my screaming daughter for another twenty minutes.

I thanked everyone and presented my papers one more time to the very grumpy man behind the desk. He corrected a few minor errors I had made on my departure card, inspected Marlee's visa packet, compared my tear-streamed face with the one on my passport, then waved me through. I grabbed my crying daughter and the handful of accessories I was carrying with me and then headed to the departure gate.

The Scotts and I had agreed to make our final separation a quiet one and not make an elaborate, emotional affair out of it for the girls' sake. As we settled into our seats on the airplane to Hong Kong, I quietly slipped away for a few moments to say my good-byes to Clyde, Maggie, Brenda and Chloe.

The flight to Hong Kong was only forty-five minutes and Marlee seemed unaffected by it all as long as I was entertaining her. I breathed a sigh of relief that my nightmare from the night before had not come true.

When we landed in Hong Kong, Elis and I intentionally took our time getting our things together before we left the plane. I wanted to give the Scotts plenty of time to go on ahead of us and get a head start so we wouldn't run into them again.

The Hong Kong airport was enormous and very modern. It seemed as if it went on for miles! Unfortunately, every flight coming in was considered international, so we had a handful of checkpoints to go through again, just like we did when we left Guangzhou.

There was a huge bottleneck at the first interview station. Murphy's Law prevailed and we ran into the Scotts. Marlee ran to Chloe the minute she saw her and threw her arms around her. No sooner had she done that when the Scotts finished their paperwork and were allowed to pass through. They scooped up Chloe and waved goodbye as casually as possible.

Marlee instantly became hysterical and started to run after Chloe. I tried to distract her, but she would have nothing to do with whatever I tempted her with. Fortunately, the Bohan family soon came upon us with their son, Caleb, who was six. They were going to be traveling on the same flight with us to San Francisco. I put my arm around Caleb and said, "Hey buddy, you're my new best friend!"

I explained to Caleb the problem and asked him if he would be willing to play with Marlee during our four hours there in Hong Kong to help take her mind off the fact that her best friend was no longer around. His chest puffed out and he acted very needed as he agreed to help me with my situation.

Three other families from our Great Wall group were traveling to San Francisco with us: the Bohans, the Biggs, and the Kerkmans. We passed through the final checkpoint along with the Biggs family, then quickly discovered how extensive the Hong Kong airport was. We received our luggage and loaded it up once again on luggage carts.

About two miles, several escalators, and an elevator later, we finally found the airline terminal that would take us back to the States. We checked our luggage once again and received our boarding passes. The very congenial airline worker explained where our plane was...a mere 65 gates away.

We still had two hours before our plane left, so we set out to find a restaurant for lunch. Laura Biggs was craving McDonald's and her husband, Terry, promised to find one for her. But after a diligent search, we realized the only McDonald's in the airport was behind us by about a thirty-minute walk.

We were all so tired, we couldn't stand the thought of retracing our steps. We all agreed that we could not eat Chinese food even one more time, so we settled for a little snack bar near our departure gate.

Since Terry had been so kind to pay for our dinner the night before at the noodle bar, I offered to pay for lunch that day. Four hot dogs, two sandwiches, a bag of chips, and four sodas came to $48 in U.S. currency. Terry admitted he got the better end of the deal.

The Bohans soon arrived at the departure gate also, and Caleb and Marlee engaged in a challenging game of football. Fortunately, the area in which we were waiting was quite spacious, so they had plenty of room to run and play. We wanted them to get their wiggles out before the long trip across the Pacific Ocean.

The football game was more of a race to see who could jump on the ball first. Caleb most always arrived first and pounced on the ball, giving him the right to throw the ball next. Marlee was getting frustrated, so I asked Caleb if he wouldn't mind allowing Marlee to get the ball once.

A few minutes later, I noticed Caleb on top of the ball with Marlee in a pile on top of him, struggling to get the ball from him. Marlee emerged from the battle with the ball in her hands and a huge smile on her face. I thanked

Caleb for allowing her to win that round and he replied, "I had to. She was hurting me."

I decided then that my plans to enroll my daughter in ballet should be augmented to include karate. She wasn't the delicate little timid flower I had envisioned. She certainly had no problem holding her own.

Twelve-thirty finally arrived and the call was made to board our flight to San Francisco. I had had about enough of boarding planes and fighting crowds. It was comforting to know there was an end in sight, but it wasn't soon enough for my liking.

We settled into our seats on the Boeing 747, about eight rows from the rear of the plane. Unfortunately, the Bohans were flying in the business section, so they were up in the front of the plane. That ruled out Caleb as Marlee's entertainment for the trip.

Even before the plane taxied for take-off, my body was screaming at me to sleep. I slipped off Marlee's shoes, pulled out her doll and blanket, and told Marlee we were going to take a nap. She put her head on my lap and I leaned back against my headrest. I couldn't wait for ten hours of sleep.

The engines roared, and we lifted off over the beautiful city of Hong Kong. Marlee lifted her head to see out the window, then instinctively looked around to see where Chloe was sitting. She stood up on the seat and called out, "Fu Chi! Fu Chi!" Her face fell when the familiar voice didn't respond, and she looked at me in bewilderment. After all, Chloe had been on every other airplane she'd been on.

I pulled her close and gave her a kiss, then explained that Chloe was with her mommy and daddy. Marlee started to cry and resisted my attempts to physically comfort her. Her antics escalated quickly, and soon she was enveloped in a full-scale tantrum. She hit, kicked, and flailed around until I could not physically hold on to her.

Thinking that it would come to a close soon, I let her get it out of her system. But the minutes turned into an hour, then the hour repeated itself, and before I knew it, she had been screaming for two hours. Nothing I did consoled her. In fact, my attempts seemed to just add fuel to the fire.

I knew the people on the plane had to be irritated by Marlee's antics. I certainly was. But as big as a 747 was, there was nowhere to escape. The only place I could think of to take her was the restroom, so I carried my kicking, screaming daughter down the aisle to the nearest bathroom.

We spent the next thirty minutes in the little three-foot square lavatory while Marlee cried, hit, and stomped. The tears streamed down her face as she screamed at me in Chinese. My heart was breaking for my little daughter who was going through such intense emotions that she didn't know how to handle.

I closed my eyes, leaned against the bathroom wall, and prayed that I would have the strength to endure the long, emotional trip ahead of us. I was exhausted already, and we still had two more flights to go. I didn't think I had the stamina to get through it. I explained to Marlee in my rough Chinese and sign language that we were not going to leave the bathroom until she stopped crying.

Finally, by some miracle, she stopped her blood-curdling scream and settled for a quiet sob. I picked her up in my arms, kissed her cheek, then exited the tiny bathroom. I walked down the aisle back to our seats and was stopped several times along the way by passengers asking if we were both alright. Without going into a lengthy explanation, I told them she was sick, tired, and had just said good-bye to her life-long best friend. Everyone showed compassion for both of us. I wasn't sure who they felt the most sorry for, me or Marlee. Elis tried to offer assistance, but Marlee would have nothing to do with her. I knew she felt helpless as well.

We had only settled into our seats for just a few minutes when Marlee started her high-intensity tantrum again. I told her that if she didn't stop, we'd go back to the bathroom. She didn't, so we did. The routine continued over several hours and we made at least a half-dozen trips to the restroom. I kept thinking that my daughter would collapse from exhaustion soon, but she just kept on going. I soon became numb, removing myself from the reality of it all and escaping into a continual state of prayer.

Occasionally, a passenger would walk by and pat me on the shoulder in an indication of support or empathy. At one point, Marlee's sobs lulled her into a somewhat stressful sleep in my arms. As long as I didn't move or try to lay her down, she slept. I sat motionless for an hour, my arms shaking under her weight and my back wrenching in pain. I didn't dare move or else she'd start screaming again. I closed my eyes and felt the tears stream down my face. I was beyond exhaustion.

We had crossed the international date line by then and time was moving backwards. Our plane had departed at 1:00 p.m., but it was the middle of the night now, several hours before we'd left. We watched the sun rise over the Pacific Ocean as we greeted Thursday, February 15th all over again. I tried to figure how long we'd been up, but my weary mind couldn't handle the task of calculating the math.

I couldn't take the frozen position I had been stuck in any longer, and needed to shift my weight to relieve my back. The movement startled Marlee and she woke up like a cranky mother bear. Her arms flailed around like a windmill as she screamed and kicked. My attempts to get her back to sleep were in vain, so it was back to the bathroom.

When we returned to our seats, a kind lady sitting two rows behind us approached me and asked if there was anything she could do to help. She explained that she spoke Mandarin Chinese and asked if she could talk with my daughter. I pleaded with her to help in any way she could. She spoke to Marlee very kindly, and for the first time in several hours, Marlee sat quietly and listened to the woman. The stranger reached out, took Marlee's hand in hers, and said, "We're going to go visit for a while. You get some rest, Mama."

I couldn't believe that I finally had a reprieve. I leaned my seat back to get some rest. It was an uneasy sleep, yet it was still sleep. I was awakened about an hour later by the kind woman who had been entertaining my daughter. She said, "Your little girl is tired and wants to come take a nap with her mama." I thanked her from the bottom of my heart for giving me those moments of relaxation.

Marlee couldn't get comfortable on my lap, so I made her a bed that stretched across both our seats and I sat on the floor in the aisle and stroked her head until she fell asleep. I desperately wanted to take advantage of the quiet and get some sleep myself.

I walked the aisles of the plane searching for an open seat, but the plane was booked and there wasn't a spare seat to be found. After the third trip around the plane, a lady waved her hand at me and offered me a seat beside her. She gave me a pillow and blanket and told me to get some rest.

I guessed I had slept for maybe twenty minutes when I was awakened by the cries of my daughter coming from several rows in front of me. I bolted out of my seat and rushed to her side. She was crying uncontrollably and reached for me. I took her in my lap and tried to console her, but her sobbing continued. It would occasionally escalate to kicking and hitting, but mostly consisted of crying and coughing.

Her throat was still incredibly sore and she would wince in pain as she cried. I had tried several times to get her to take the antibiotic the doctor had prescribed, but she would have nothing to do with it. After having it spit all over me several times, I quit trying to give it to her.

Amazingly, the few moments of rest I was able to get were enough to give me the energy I needed to handle Marlee's antics for the rest of the flight. Finally, at 9:00 a.m. United States Pacific time, we landed at the San Francisco International Airport, ten and one-half hours after we left Hong Kong.

THE GOOD OL' USA

I'm sure the passengers of flight 603 were more than elated when we landed. They had all been incredibly supportive throughout the miserable flight, but I'm sure the thought of not having to listen to a screaming child gave them peace. Marlee was exhausted from her ten-hour tantrum and insisted I carry her from the plane.

It was 11:00 p.m. to us, but in San Francisco, the day was just beginning. We walked down a large corridor to the area where international flights arrived. Several signs lit up over our heads indicating which line we were to stand in. We were instructed to go to the "New Immigrant" line, since Marlee was immigrating to the United States from China. The lines were long and they moved slowly. Marlee was ecstatic to be off the plane and she ran around with excitement. I kept having to leave

my place in line to capture her and bring her back.

Our turn finally came to show our passports, Marlee's

visa, and all the adoption documentation. After

everything was approved by an immigration official, we

were escorted to the INS office there at the airport. A

very personable lady reviewed Marlee's documents and

opened the all-important visa envelope I had been

carrying with me since the ceremony at the U.S.

Consulate. It was a little crumpled from the long journey,

but everything was still intact. She stamped Marlee's

passport and told me that was her clearance to obtain a

social security card. She wished us well and welcomed us

back to the States.

Just outside the INS office was the international

baggage claim. We joined the hundreds of other people

on our flight in distinguishing which luggage was ours. Marlee thought that was great fun and ran up and down the aisle of luggage saying, "This one? This one?"

We found our luggage and passed through customs without any major difficulties. Fortunately, the check-in for our flight to Seattle was not far away and we didn't have to push our mountain of luggage any great distance.

We gave the attendant our tickets and received our boarding passes in return. Seeing the word "Seattle" on the pass made my heart ache for home. We said our good-byes to the Bohans and Biggs, who were headed for Texas. We had become quite good friends in the two weeks we'd spent together, and it was hard to say farewell to them.

Wearily we made our way through the crowds to our departure gate for Seattle. When we arrived, we discovered that our flight had been cancelled, therefore we would be taking an earlier flight to Seattle in just one hour.

I took Marlee to the restroom nearby so we could both freshen up a little before our next flight. It was her first encounter with an American bathroom, and she was completely intrigued by the modern facilities of the United States. She looked all around to find the handle to flush the toilet, then looked at me in bewilderment. Just then the toilet made the whooshing sound as it flushed automatically. Marlee jumped back in surprise and looked at me as if some type of magic had just occurred. I reassured her everything was okay and escorted her to the sinks to wash her hands.

Once again, she was amazed by automation. She put her little hands under the faucet and the water immediately poured over them. She looked up at me again in awe, then pulled her hands away. The water stopped. A smile came across her face and she promptly stuck her hands back under the faucet, then out again. She giggled at her newly found discovery and I let her entertain herself for a few minutes.

I finally coaxed her away from the sink and led her to yet another fantastic invention, the automatic hand dryer. She dried her hands, arms, face, hair, and legs. Everything she could think of, she dried.

I finally told her it was time to go and started out of the restroom. When I looked behind me to ensure Marlee was in tow, she was back at the sink washing her hands again. She went through the wash-your-hands, dry-your-body routine at least four times before I finally dragged her out of the restroom. We were just in time to hear the call to board our early flight. With a renewed energy, the three of us settled in to the eighth flight of our trip.

San Francisco was spectacular that day, and the view of the Bay was incredible. We had barely reached cruising altitude before Marlee snuggled her head in my lap and was snoring loudly. Elis and I gave each other a quiet high five and reclined back in our seats for one hour and forty-five minutes of quiet relaxation.

It's amazing how time flies when you're sleeping. No sooner had I closed my eyes when I heard the pilot announce we were landing in Seattle. I couldn't believe we were there already! Couldn't they just circle the airport for another eight hours so we could all finish our naps? It was just after noon, but I calculated it to be 4:00 a.m. China time.

I waited until the very last minute to wake my beautiful, sleeping daughter. She opened her eyes and came up swinging. She was completely irritated that she had been awakened and intended to let everyone know so. I struggled to carry her from the plane as Elis juggled all of our carry-on luggage.

Even though we were still two hundred miles from the Tri-Cities, it still felt like we were home. Seattle was close enough in my book, and it was like putting on my favorite pair of sweatpants and slippers when I walked into the Sea-Tac Airport. We had arrived an hour early, so I didn't expect the friends and family I had invited to meet us to be there yet. We found the nearest ladies restroom and we all freshened up after our short nap from San Francisco.

At 1:15 we wandered back to our arrival gate since our scheduled arrival time in Seattle was 1:30 p.m. My friend, Chris, was going to meet us there and visit with us during our four-hour layover. I had intentionally scheduled the long stay there in Seattle in order to have time with Chris, tell her about our trip, and give her a chance to meet Marlee. My parents were also in Seattle that week and I had invited them to come meet their new granddaughter rather than wait three more days until they returned home.

The clock ticked away. The hands passed 1:30, then on to 2:00. I looked around the entire waiting area to see a familiar face, but I didn't see anyone. I finally conceded that none of them had been able to make it, so we took Marlee, who was still throwing the tantrum of the century, down the corridor to an eating area with several restaurants.

One thing we hadn't had in over two weeks was a good old-fashioned hamburger. The Burger King sign seemed to call our names, and we found a comfortable place to land on some cushioned benches.

I stood in line to order and could hear my irate daughter clear across the eating area of the airport. When I finally arrived with the food, she was staring at me in a type of comatose trance. If she could have spoken fluent English, I'm sure she would have said, "Mom, you've been dragging me across the world for the last day and a half. If you put me on one more airplane, I'm going to die! Let me go to sleep now and nobody will get hurt!"

I tried to entice her with a cheeseburger and french fries, but she only ate a few bites half-heartedly. Her eyes rolled back in her head, then she slowly slid down the back of the bench. Her body toppled over to the side, where her weary head rested on her blanket. She flopped one arm over her eyes and yelled at me angrily when I tried to remove her shoes and make her more comfortable. Her eyes were closed, but occasionally she would kick her legs and pound her feet and yell what I was sure to be some type of Chinese obscenity at me.

Elis opted to take a walk around the airport to kill time, and I didn't blame her for that choice. I would have rather licked the airport floor clean with my tongue than spend another three hours with my out-of-control daughter. But I was the mommy and didn't have the option of getting away. I cleared away the burgers and fries we didn't eat and laid my head down on the table. Marlee was even snoring in a grumpy tone.

I set my pager alarm for 4:15 p.m. since we needed to be at our departure gate by 4:30. I tried to rest, but the fatigue that penetrated my body made me physically sick. I struggled many times to keep from vomiting. I wondered what I would do if I had to throw up, because I couldn't leave Marlee asleep on a restaurant bench in the middle of a large international airport.

I sat and contemplated the pros and cons of asking a stranger to watch her while I ran to the bathroom and puked or just going ahead and hurling right there in the middle of the restaurant. Either way it wasn't pretty. I finally just retrieved one of the paper Burger King bags and resigned myself to using the bag if need be. I had to stick my face in it a couple times, but just resorted to gagging instead of completely tossing my lunch. I lay with my head on the table and my eyes closed, wishing someone would just shoot me and put me out of my misery. My body shook with exhaustion as I fought back the dry heaves.

Twenty short minutes after I was able to relax enough to go to sleep, my alarm went off. Elis had just returned from her expedition and helped me gather our things for our final flight home.

THE HOMECOMING

It was a very cold day in Seattle and the forecast was snow. I carefully took my sleeping daughter in my arms and carried her to our final flight. The wind kissed us with a cold smack. I pulled Marlee's pink blanket up over her head to shield her from the cold, but the bitter wind woke her up with a start. "The party's over," I thought to myself. I was all geared up for another tantrum.

In front of us on the runway were six airplanes lined up in a row. The airline attendant looked at our passes and held his arm straight out as he pointed with his finger. "Yours is the very last one."

I shot him a glance that implied every obscenity I'd ever heard. I was wishing he would see the frustration and exhaustion in my face and say, "Oh, please let me carry your heavy, grumpy daughter for you. You look so weary from your long journey and I wouldn't want you to have a nervous breakdown this close to home." But he just stood there and smiled at me. I made a mental note to cross him off my Christmas card list.

Surprisingly, Marlee just raised her head up and looked around instead of screaming. I almost toppled over backwards as I climbed up the small stairs to the entrance of the airplane. The weight of carrying Marlee halfway around the world had finally done me in. My back was screaming at me.

Each of our airplanes had become progressively smaller as we got closer to home. This last one had a whopping sixteen seats. Marlee and I sat beside each other in the front two seats. She looked up at me and winced when the propellers started. I held up my index finger and said, "Just one more airplane, then we will see Ba Ba and Ge Ge."

Marlee's eyes widened as she said, "Ba Ba?" She held up her index finger and indicated she understood we were finally on our last flight. A smile graced her lips and she looked out the window at Seattle disappearing underneath us. I pulled out her markers and paper and we traced her hand several times. We sang a few songs, ate the snacks the attendant gave us, then finally heard the pilot announce that we were descending into Pasco. The time was 5:45 p.m.

The wheels of the airplane had barely touched down when Marlee started shouting, "Ba Ba! Ba Ba!" She struggled to get out of her seat and I had to pin her down until the plane came to a stop.

The airplane door opened and we were met by huge snowflakes dancing and swirling outside. All the passengers had learned our story in the fifty minutes it took to fly from Seattle to Pasco, so they cordially let us exit the plane first.

I carried Marlee through the snowflakes across the tarmac to the sliding doors that opened into the airport. I heard someone say, "Here they are!" Dozens of people rushed around to hold up welcome signs and balloons. They clapped as we entered and I stopped just inside the doors to wave at everyone and take it all in.

Tim and Eric stood just a few feet in front of us, Eric holding a giant Panda. I carried Marlee over to meet the rest of her new family. I gave Eric a big hug and a kiss and introduced Marlee to her big brother. He knelt down and looked at her eye to eye as Marlee smiled and hugged me tight.

I scooped Marlee up in my arms as she held onto me. Tim came forward and kissed me, then looked down into the face of his new daughter. I placed my hand on his chest and patted it. "This is Ba Ba", I repeated over and over. She looked up at him with an overwhelmed awe in her eyes. She smiled and didn't say a word.

I looked around to see over fifty friends and family members surrounding us with signs, balloons, gifts, and tears. I made my way through the crowd with Marlee on my hip, giving hugs and kisses to everyone who had come to great us. Tim and Eric followed beside us.

John Trumbo from the Tri-City Herald was there to greet us and held a short interview with me, asking about our stay in China and the trip home. Deb Nelson from

KVEW television was also there and stayed until we were all done with our welcoming before she asked several questions of us also.

Finally, after over thirty minutes of fanfare, the crowd slowly dissipated and we went down to claim our luggage. Marlee finally let me put her down and Eric took her by the hand as he guided her to the baggage claim area.

Elis was waiting there with my brother and sister-in-law. I threw my arms around Elis, broke into tears, and thanked her from the bottom of my heart for all her help in our adventure. I couldn't have done it without her.

Friends gathered up my luggage and escorted us out of the airport. When we reached the doors to leave into the cold night air, Tim held his hands out to Marlee and said, "Can Ba Ba carry you to the car?" Marlee raised her head and looked up at her new daddy, then lifted her arms in approval. I could see Tim's face melt as he reached down and scooped up his new daughter in his arms. Marlee wrapped one arm around his neck while she stroked his goatee with the other hand. It was apparently love at first sight for both of them.

Tim carefully placed Marlee into her car seat in the back. He showed her the buckles he was going to fasten across her shoulders and between her legs. I anticipated a royal resistance, but she let him secure her without any struggle. I sat beside her and held her hand to offer comfort.

I sat for a moment before the car started and took in the scene I was finally a part of. The little girl I had visualized for so many years was now a reality. She was a part of our family. The vacant seat in the back of the car, the empty chair at the dinner table, and the hole in the family picture—they were now filled.

Marlee reached toward the front passenger where Eric was sitting and insisted that he hold her hand. He obliged by stretching his hand as far back as he could to reach her. She grasped his hand with her left hand, while still holding mine with her right. She looked at me with a smile I had never seen before on her face. It radiated peace, comfort and security. Her face implied the words, "This is what I've been waiting for. I'm with my family now and we're going home."

Tim drove as if he was chauffeuring the armored car that carried the Hope Diamond. Every corner and every bump was taken with extreme caution. It seemed like it took forever to drive the short nine miles from the airport to our home. The snowflakes that were still falling made it a challenge to see through the black night sky.

Eric tried desperately to conceal his tears as he sobbed in the front seat. When I asked him what was wrong he replied, "I'm just so happy. I've waited for this moment for ten years and I can't believe it's here. I'm just so happy she's here."

As we pulled into our driveway, I breathed a sigh of relief. It seemed like a lifetime ago that I had left behind my family and boarded that first plane heading for China. So much had happened in the fourteen days I had been gone from home.

We escorted Marlee into the house and took her from room to room introducing her to her new surroundings. She loved her bedroom that held her dollhouse, vanity, stuffed animals, and a closet and dresser full of more clothes than one little girl should have. Although she seemed intrigued by it, I didn't think she realized that it was all actually hers. After all, she'd never had anything that ever belonged to her, so immediately understanding the ownership concept was something I didn't expect her to grasp.

I changed both our clothes from the ones we'd been in for the last thirty-three hours. It felt incredible to put on my favorite pair of sweatpants and sweatshirt. I dressed Marlee in a pink flowered outfit I had purchased before the trip and showed her the Minnie Mouse slippers she had received as a shower gift. Her eyes lit up as she shouted, "Minnie!"

By the time we had freshened up, Tim had unloaded the car and my luggage was spread out over the entire living room floor. I couldn't believe I had actually hauled

Shannon G. Turner

all that stuff half way around the world! We sat down in the middle of it all and Marlee and I started distributing the gifts we had brought for Tim and Eric. We showed them everything we had purchased and told them stories about our trip.

When we finished, it was Tim and Eric's turn to present gifts. After I had explained my unsuccessful attempts to purchase a ball in China, Tim and Eric went out and bought every ball they could find. Marlee was in ball heaven! She and Eric played together for the first time as brother and sister. Tim and I watched our children play as if it was a fairy tale that had finally come true.

It wasn't long before our second wind began to taper off rapidly. It was almost 9:00 p.m. and my body felt as if I could sleep for a week. I explained to Marlee in Chinese

374

that it was time for bed. She instantly reached her hands up for Tim to carry her up the stairs. Again his face melted.

I dressed Marlee in the new pajamas Tim had bought for her that day. Tim could barely speak the words of his prayer as he thanked our Heavenly Father for this wonderful gift He had given us. He ended the prayer and Marlee pronounced a very clear, "Amen."

Marlee reached down and gathered the covers in her hands, then flopped back with her head on her pillow. She gathered the blankets up under her chin, wiggled a couple times to get settled, then closed her eyes. The most beautiful smile I had ever seen graced her little face. It said, "I'm home."

Our little miracle from China was finally home.

NOTES

1. "The character for mei combines..."

   Barbara Aria with Russell Eng Gon, *The Spirit of the Chinese Character, Gifts from the Heart*, (New York: Running Heads Incorporated, 1992)

2. "Somewhere Out There..."

   Somewhere Out There, Words and music by Barry Mann, Cynthia Weil, and James Horner.

3. "No pain that we suffer..."

   Orson F. Whitney, in Dennis D. Flake, "Orson F. Whitney's Philosophy of Education," p. 96; see also Spencer W. Kimball, *Faith Precedes the Miracle*, p. 99

4. "It shows what..."

Gordon B. Hinckley, Deseret News, Jun. 30, 2001, 6.

ABOUT THE AUTHOR

Shannon Turner lives in the Tri-Cities area of Washington State with her husband and children. Living only six blocks from her parents' home where she grew up, she keeps her extended family close to her and enjoys frequent activities with them. Shannon is the Crime Specialist/Evidence Technician with the Pasco Police Department, having worked in the criminal justice system over twenty years. She has enjoyed writing since she was a child, having had many teachers comment that she had a gift for writing and a unique sense of humor. She has played the cello since age nine and has performed with many symphonies and local production companies. She enjoys arranging solos and duets to perform for church and civic events.

Printed in the United States
22795LVS00003B/73-78

9 781403 366313